LIFE LESSONS
FROM THE
GREAT MINDS

Curated Wisdom on Love, Happiness, and Meaning

FELIX GRAYSON

MINDSPARK
PUBLISHING

To the seekers, the dreamers, and the resilient hearts who dare to live with purpose and love with courage—this book is for you.

"What you leave behind is not what is engraved in stone monuments, but what is woven into the lives of others."

— Pericles

ABOUT STONED PHILOSOPHER

Welcome to the *Stoned Philosopher* series—where timeless wisdom meets the modern world.

Each book distills powerful lessons from history's greatest minds, leaders, and thinkers—transforming their ideas into practical insights for today's challenges.

From mastering habits, calm, and resilience to understanding success, leadership, and meaning, this collection invites you to think deeper, live wiser, and see life from new perspectives.

Whether you're exploring *Modern Zen*, uncovering *The Wisdom of Warriors*, or seeking clarity through *The Art of Perspective*, every title offers a journey toward self-mastery and understanding.

Discover the full *Stoned Philosopher* collection and more at **FelixGrayson.com**, home of **Mind-Spark Publishing**—where knowledge, philosophy, and storytelling come together to spark lifelong curiosity.

Wisdom isn't something we find—it's something we grow into.

Let the journey begin.

CONTENTS

INTRODUCTION: A JOURNEY THROUGH THE WISDOM OF GREAT MINDS 10

CHAPTER 1: THE PURSUIT OF LOVE – LESSONS ON CONNECTION AND COMPASSION 18

The Nature of Love Across History 19

Self-Love as the Foundation 24

Building Healthy Connections 29

Love as a Unifying Force 36

CHAPTER 2: THE ART OF HAPPINESS – INSIGHTS ON JOY AND CONTENTMENT 43

Philosophical Definitions of Happiness 44

The Role of Gratitude and Perspective 49

Living in Alignment with Values 55

Inner Peace in a Chaotic World 62

CHAPTER 3: FINDING PURPOSE – THE SEARCH FOR MEANING IN LIFE 68

The Eternal Quest for Meaning 69

Aligning Purpose with Action 75

Contribution and Service to Others 81

Small Moments, Big Purpose 87

CHAPTER 4: RESILIENCE OF THE HUMAN SPIRIT – LESSONS ON OVERCOMING ADVERSITY 94

The Philosophy of Suffering and Growth 95

Lessons from Great Lives 100

The Role of Mindset in Adversity 107

Overcoming Personal Obstacles 114

CHAPTER 5: LIVING AUTHENTICALLY – THE COURAGE TO BE YOURSELF 121

Philosophical Foundations of Authenticity 122

Rejecting Conformity and External Expectations .. 128

The Power of Vulnerability 134

Authenticity in Action 141

CHAPTER 6: THE POWER OF CONNECTION – LESSONS ON BUILDING COMMUNITY AND BELONGING 148

The Importance of Human Connection 149

Building Meaningful Relationships 155

Creating and Leading Communities 162

The Role of Empathy and Compassion 168

CHAPTER 7: REFLECTIONS ON MORTALITY – EMBRACING LIFE BY ACCEPTING DEATH 176

Philosophers on the Nature of Death 177

Living Fully Through Awareness of Mortality 182

Overcoming the Fear of Death 189

Leaving Nothing Unsaid 195

CHAPTER 8: THE LEGACY WE LEAVE – LESSONS ON CONTRIBUTION AND IMPACT 201

Defining Legacy Through Timeless Teachings 202

Acts of Service and Kindness 208

Creating Meaningful Work 214

Your Legacy Begins Now 220

CONCLUSION: EMBRACING THE JOURNEY OF A MEANINGFUL LIFE 227

INTRODUCTION: A JOURNEY THROUGH THE WISDOM OF GREAT MINDS

What does it mean to live a meaningful life? This question, as old as humanity itself, has echoed through the minds of philosophers, poets, and visionaries for centuries. From the bustling agora of ancient Athens to the quiet retreats of Zen monasteries, from the fiery speeches of revolutionaries to the gentle counsel of sages, the search for purpose and fulfillment has been a universal pursuit. And while the answers vary—shaped by culture, time, and individual experience—the questions remain timeless: How do we find happiness? How do we navigate suffering? How do we live authentically, connect deeply, and leave a legacy that matters?

This book is an invitation to explore these questions through the lens of history's greatest thinkers and leaders. It is not a manual or a prescription but a journey—one that weaves together the threads of philosophy, psychology, and human experience to illuminate the timeless lessons that guide us toward a life of meaning and impact.

As you turn these pages, you will walk alongside figures like Socrates and Confucius, Marcus Aurelius and the Buddha, Leonardo da Vinci and Mother Teresa. Their lives and teachings, though separated by centuries and continents, share a common thread: a profound understanding of what it means to live well. They remind us that the path to fulfillment is not found in fleeting achievements or external accolades but in the choices we make, the values we uphold, and the connections we nurture.

The Power of Timeless Wisdom

In today's fast-paced, hyperconnected world, the wisdom of the past might seem irrelevant or outdated. After all, what can an ancient Roman emperor or a 13th-century Persian poet teach us about navigating the complexities of modern life? The answer, as you will discover, is everything.

The challenges we face today—stress, uncertainty, loneliness, and a yearning for purpose—are not new. They are the same struggles that have shaped human experience for millennia. What has changed are the tools and technologies at our disposal, the pace of our lives, and the noise that often distracts us from what truly matters. In this whirlwind of modern existence, the teachings of great minds offer a quiet, steady voice—a reminder to slow down, to reflect, and to focus on what endures.

This book is a bridge between past and present, a guide that distills the profound insights of history into practical lessons for today. Each chapter explores a central theme—love, happiness, resilience, authenticity, connection, mortality, and legacy—drawing on the wisdom of thinkers and leaders who have grappled with these universal questions. Their reflections, combined with contemporary insights, provide a roadmap for navigating the complexities of life with clarity, courage, and grace.

Why This Journey Matters

The purpose of this book is not merely to inform

but to transform. It is not enough to understand the principles of a meaningful life; we must embody them. The teachings of Confucius, Marcus Aurelius, and Viktor Frankl, among others, challenge us to look inward, to examine our beliefs and habits, and to align our actions with our highest values.

Consider, for a moment, the idea of legacy. Legacy is not something we leave behind at the end of our lives; it is something we build every day. It is found in the love we give, the work we create, and the impact we have on others. To live with this awareness is to approach each moment with intention, knowing that our choices—no matter how small—shape the world around us.

This is the heart of the book: an invitation to live fully, authentically, and courageously. It is a call to embrace the wisdom of the past not as an abstract ideal but as a practical guide for the present.

What You Will Discover

Each chapter of this book is a step on the journey, exploring a key aspect of a meaningful life through the lens of philosophy, history, and human experience:

- In Chapter 1, you will delve into the nature of love and connection, discovering how the teachings of Plato, Rumi, and others illuminate the profound power of compassion and relationships.

- In Chapter 2, you will explore the art of happiness, learning how gratitude, perspective, and mindfulness can transform your experience of joy.

- In Chapter 3, you will reflect on the search for purpose, guided by the insights of Nietzsche, Lao Tzu, and Viktor Frankl.

- In Chapter 4, you will uncover the resilience of the human spirit, drawing strength from the stories of Nelson Mandela and Helen Keller.

- In Chapter 5, you will examine the courage to live authentically, inspired by the wisdom of Socrates, Emerson, and Brené Brown.

- In Chapter 6, you will embrace the power of

connection, exploring how community and empathy shape our lives and the world.

- In Chapter 7, you will confront mortality, learning how to live fully by accepting life's impermanence.

- In Chapter 8, you will reflect on legacy, discovering how small, intentional acts of kindness and purpose leave a lasting impact.

Each chapter is not an ending but a beginning, offering insights and tools to help you navigate your own journey.

The Path Ahead

As you embark on this journey, remember that the wisdom of great minds is not a set of rules but a source of inspiration. It is a compass, not a map. Each of us must chart our own course, guided by our values, experiences, and aspirations.

This book is not about perfection. It is about progress. It is about recognizing that we are all works in progress, that the journey toward a meaningful life is not a destination but an on-going practice. Whether you are seeking clarity in times of uncertainty, strength in moments of struggle, or a deeper sense of purpose, the insights within these pages are here to support you.

As the poet Rumi wrote, "Be like a tree and let the dead leaves drop." These words remind us that growth requires letting go—of fear, of doubt, of the need to have all the answers. To embrace the wisdom of the past is to open our-selves to new possibilities, to trust in the process of becoming, and to step forward with courage and hope.

An Invitation

This book is not merely about learning; it is about living. It is an invitation to reflect on your values, to cultivate love and resilience, to con-nect deeply with others, and to leave a legacy that matters.

As you read these pages, I encourage you to approach them with curiosity and openness. Let the stories and insights resonate with your own experiences. Reflect on the questions that arise, and consider how the lessons of great minds can enrich your own life.

Above all, remember that this journey is yours. The wisdom of the past is a gift, but the choices you make today are what truly define your path. So as you begin this book, take a moment to ask yourself: What kind of life do I want to create? What impact do I want to have? And what steps can I take, right now, to align my actions with my highest aspirations?

The answers may not come all at once, but the journey itself is where meaning is found. Let this book be your companion and guide as you embark on the adventure of a lifetime: the adventure of living fully, authentically, and with purpose.

Welcome to the journey. It begins here.

CHAPTER 1: THE PURSUIT OF LOVE – LESSONS ON CONNECTION AND COMPASSION

The Nature of Love Across History

Love, that most ancient and mysterious of human emotions, has shaped civilizations, inspired poetry, and perplexed even the greatest minds. Across time, thinkers and philosophers have sought to define its essence, distinguish its forms, and understand its purpose. To Plato, Rumi, and Confucius—figures who stood at the crossroads of wisdom and culture—love was not a single feeling but a spectrum of connection, desire, and compassion that illuminated the human experience. Their interpretations, though born centuries apart, resonate with timeless truths, providing us with guidance on how to love well—ourselves, others, and the world.

Plato, the Athenian philosopher whose dialogues laid the groundwork for much of Western thought, explored love not as mere passion or physical attraction but as a transformative force. In *The Symposium*, one of his most profound works, Plato presents love as a ladder—a journey that begins with physical desire and ascends to a higher appreciation of beauty itself. This concept, known as "Platonic love," emphasized that while physical attraction may spark connection, true love transcends it. For Plato, the purest form of love was not about possession but about nurturing the soul of the other, helping one another realize their highest potential.

This vision of love as a path toward the divine — toward truth, wisdom, and virtue — offers us an enduring lesson: love is not static. It is a journey of growth. In today's world, where relationships are often reduced to fleeting digital interactions or superficial bonds, Plato's insight invites us to approach love with intention. Whether romantic or platonic, our relationships can be fertile ground for mutual transformation, a place where both individuals aspire to become their best selves. The question is: Are we willing to climb that ladder, to move beyond our own desires and help others ascend alongside us?

While Plato's love emphasized the mind's elevation, Rumi, the 13th-century Persian mystic and poet, infused love with spiritual ecstasy. To Rumi, love was not a philosophical idea but a force of divine connection — a thread that binds all beings to one another and to the sacred. In his verses, love is both fire and water, destruction and creation. It is through love, Rumi believed, that we come closest to God and to understanding our place in the universe. "Let yourself be silently drawn by the strange pull of what you really love. It will not lead you astray," he wrote, encapsulating the idea that love is a compass guiding us toward meaning.

Unlike Plato, who described love as a gradual climb, Rumi presented it as an all-encompassing surrender. His poetry teaches us to embrace vulnerability in love, to let go of ego, and to open our hearts fully—even if it means experiencing pain. "Don't grieve," he writes. "Anything you lose comes round in another form." Love, in Rumi's vision, is eternal, and its purpose is not to possess but to dissolve the boundaries between self and other. Here lies a modern application: To truly love, we must let go of control. We must trust that love, like water, will flow where it needs to, healing the wounds it touches and nourishing the roots of our relationships.

Across the world in ancient China, Confucius— one of history's greatest moral philosophers— approached love as the foundation of ethical living. For Confucius, love was not abstract but practical, expressed through *ren*, a concept often translated as "benevolence" or "human-heartedness." *Ren* was the thread that wove together familial piety, respect for others, and social harmony. Love, according to Confucius, began within the family unit. To honor and care for one's parents and siblings was the first act of love; from this foundation, one could extend compassion outward, fostering a just and peaceful society.

Confucius' teachings challenge the modern narrative of love as solely personal or romantic. In our hyper-individualistic world, where love is often confined to intimate relationships, his vision broadens our perspective. Love, Confucius reminds us, is a civic duty—a force that binds families, communities, and nations. By practicing love within our closest circles, we create ripples of harmony that extend far beyond ourselves. His wisdom remains profoundly relevant: In fractured societies plagued by division and mistrust, love expressed through compassion, respect, and responsibility can be the glue that holds us together.

What unites these thinkers—Plato, Rumi, and

Confucius—is their shared belief that love, in all its forms, is transformative. For Plato, it is the vehicle through which we ascend toward truth and beauty. For Rumi, it is the force that unites us with the divine. For Confucius, it is the practice of benevolence that sustains relationships and society. Though their cultural and temporal contexts differ, they converge on one point: Love is not passive. It requires effort, vulnerability, and action.

Today, their wisdom invites us to reimagine love as more than a fleeting emotion or transactional exchange. It asks us to nurture relationships with purpose, to view love as a journey that strengthens our character, expands our understanding of others, and brings meaning to our lives. The nature of love—romantic, familial, and universal—is vast and complex, but at its core, it is a bridge that connects us to the world, to each other, and to something greater than ourselves.

In modern relationships, we can embody Plato's call for growth, Rumi's surrender to vulnerability, and Confucius' commitment to benevolence. By doing so, we honor the timeless wisdom of history's great minds, transforming love from something we feel into something we actively give and live.

Self-Love as the Foundation

The idea of self-love often conjures images of indulgence or self-centeredness in a world that prizes productivity and external validation. Yet, when viewed through the lens of ancient wisdom and modern psychology, self-love emerges not as selfishness but as the bedrock of meaningful relationships and inner fulfillment. To love others authentically, one must first learn to embrace and nurture oneself. Aristotle, one of the greatest thinkers in history, considered self-love not just a virtue but the very foundation of a flourishing life. Modern psychologists echo this sentiment, highlighting that without self-compassion and a healthy relationship with oneself, our capacity to love and connect with others remains stunted.

Aristotle's understanding of self-love was profound and practical. In his *Nicomachean Ethics*, he described self-love as an essential component of *eudaimonia*—the state of living well or achieving true happiness. Unlike narcissism, which feeds on ego and external admiration, Aristotle's self-love was deeply tied to virtue. To love oneself, he argued, is to act in accordance with one's highest values and moral principles. A person who truly loves themselves seeks to be good, not for applause or validation, but because goodness is an intrinsic part of a fulfilling life.

Aristotle's message carries a modern resonance: self-love is not a fleeting feeling of worthiness but a commitment to cultivating the best version of oneself. It demands self-respect, self-awareness, and the courage to confront one's flaws and shortcomings without judgment. In our hyper-connected, social media-driven culture, where the need for external validation often eclipses self-reflection, Aristotle's wisdom invites us to return inward. Self-love begins with asking: What kind of person do I want to become? And more importantly, am I living in alignment with that vision?

The modern psychologist Carl Rogers, one of the founders of humanistic psychology, built upon this classical idea by emphasizing the role of self-acceptance in personal growth. Rogers believed that individuals flourish when they experience "unconditional positive regard"—a profound acceptance of oneself, regardless of imperfections or past failures. He noted that the people most capable of loving others were those who had first learned to accept themselves, flaws and all. To Rogers, self-love was a prerequisite for genuine human connection. If we are constantly at war with ourselves, we project that internal conflict onto our relationships, turning love into something transactional or conditional.

Self-love, therefore, is not indulgence; it is liberation. It frees us from the endless cycle of seeking external approval and allows us to offer love to others without strings attached. To care for ourselves—whether through cultivating habits that nourish the body, prioritizing emotional well-being, or setting boundaries—becomes an act of radical self-respect. It is not an escape from responsibility to others but rather the foundation from which all love flows.

Consider the parable of the overflowing cup, a metaphor found in both Eastern and Western traditions. The cup represents our inner resources—our energy, compassion, and capacity for connection. When the cup is empty, we have little to offer others. Relationships become strained, and our acts of love feel forced or performative. But when we fill our own cup—through self-care, self-reflection, and kindness to ourselves—love overflows naturally. This is the essence of Aristotle's and Rogers' teachings: self-love enables us to give more freely, not less.

The practice of self-love also requires courage. In many ways, it demands that we stand against cultural norms that equate self-worth with productivity, perfection, or sacrifice. History provides us with examples of individuals who embodied this courage—figures who recognized that loving oneself was a necessary step toward a greater purpose. Eleanor Roosevelt, for example, spoke often of her journey toward self-respect. "No one can make you feel inferior without your consent," she famously said, reflecting the belief that true strength begins with self-acceptance. Roosevelt understood that in order to serve others—whether through leadership or compassion—she had to first believe in her own intrinsic worth.

In Eastern traditions, this concept of self-love manifests as self-compassion. Buddhist teachings, for example, emphasize *metta*, or loving-kindness, as a practice that begins inward and radiates outward. "You, yourself, as much as anybody in the entire universe, deserve your love and affection," the Buddha taught, emphasizing that compassion is incomplete if we exclude ourselves from its embrace. In modern psychology, this same principle is echoed by Dr. Kristin Neff, who identifies self-compassion as the antidote to self-criticism. Neff encourages individuals to treat themselves as they would a close friend—offering understanding, patience, and kindness rather than harsh judgment.

For readers navigating modern life, where pressures to achieve, conform, or meet impossible standards abound, the wisdom of Aristotle, Rogers, and the Buddha offers a roadmap to self-love. It begins not with grand gestures but with small, intentional acts: forgiving oneself for mistakes, resting when the body and mind demand it, and choosing actions that reflect one's values. Self-love requires us to challenge the voice of self-criticism and replace it with one of compassion.

Practical applications of self-love are varied but deeply personal. For some, it may mean prioritizing time for reflection or creative expression. For others, it might involve setting healthy boundaries in relationships or stepping away from environments that drain emotional energy. Regardless of the form it takes, the underlying truth remains the same: when we treat ourselves with the same care and understanding we offer those we love, we create the foundation for more authentic, meaningful connections with others.

Ultimately, self-love is not an endpoint but an ongoing practice. It is a daily commitment to honor one's worth, embrace imperfection, and act in ways that align with one's highest good. In the words of Aristotle, "All friendly feelings for others are an extension of man's feelings for himself." To love others deeply and compassionately, we must first learn to love the person in the mirror. Only then can love become the unshakable force that builds relationships, heals wounds, and brings meaning to our lives.

Building Healthy Connections

Human beings are wired for connection. From the smallest communities to the largest empires, the strength of human bonds has determined the success of families, societies, and civilizations. Yet, as fundamental as relationships are to our existence, they remain among the most complex and misunderstood aspects of human life. Great thinkers throughout history have pondered what it means to build and sustain strong, meaningful connections. Marcus Aurelius, the Roman Emperor and Stoic philosopher, offers particularly timeless wisdom on this matter, emphasizing trust, empathy, and communication as the cornerstones of healthy relationships.

Marcus Aurelius ruled at a time of immense challenges—wars, plagues, and internal unrest—yet his *Meditations*, a personal journal of reflections, reveals a deep commitment to understanding and improving human relationships. He believed that individuals are inherently social beings, interdependent by nature. "Human beings have been made for one another. Teach them or bear with them," he wrote. This simple yet profound insight highlights two essential truths:

first, that we need each other to thrive, and second, that imperfection is inevitable. Healthy relationships, therefore, are built on both effort and patience—a willingness to guide others with kindness while accepting their flaws with grace.

Marcus Aurelius teaches us that trust is the foundation upon which all connections are built. Without trust, relationships become transactional, fraught with suspicion and resentment. Trust, however, is not something granted unconditionally; it is earned through consistent actions, honesty, and reliability. To foster trust, one must live with integrity, aligning words with actions and honoring commitments. For Marcus, integrity was not merely a personal virtue but a relational one—it signaled to others that they were safe, respected, and valued.

Empathy, too, sits at the heart of meaningful relationships. Marcus Aurelius reminds us that we each carry invisible burdens. "Whenever you are about to find fault with someone, ask yourself the following question: What fault of mine most nearly resembles the one I am about to criticize?" This exercise in humility and empathy encourages us to look inward before passing judgment, recognizing that we are all flawed and fallible. By seeing the humanity in others — their struggles, fears, and desires — we move beyond surface-level connections and create space for deeper understanding. Empathy allows us to replace judgment with compassion, criticism with support. It transforms relationships into places of safety and mutual growth.

The practice of empathy has practical applications in modern life. In a world often characterized by superficial interactions, taking the time to truly listen — to understand another person's perspective without rushing to respond or fix — can be a revolutionary act. The 20th-century philosopher Martin Buber captured this idea in his concept of "I-Thou" relationships. Buber argued that meaningful relationships arise when we see others not as objects or means to an end but as unique, sacred beings worthy of our full attention and respect. When we approach conversations with curiosity rather than assumption, we cultivate empathy and create bonds that are authentic and enduring.

Communication, the third pillar of healthy relationships, was central not only to Stoic philosophy but to the teachings of thinkers like Aristotle and modern psychologists. Marcus Aurelius believed that words held immense power—not just to convey ideas but to build or destroy connections. "Give yourself a gift: the present moment," he wrote, urging readers to practice mindfulness in their interactions. Clear, honest communication rooted in kindness allows us to express our needs, resolve misunderstandings, and foster connection without causing harm.

Today, the art of communication is often lost amid distractions and digital noise. Text messages replace meaningful conversations, and misunderstandings multiply in the absence of tone and presence. To build strong relationships, we must return to the basics: listening actively, speaking truthfully, and choosing words that uplift rather than tear down. Psychologists emphasize the importance of "active listening"—a practice that involves giving someone our full attention, reflecting back what we hear, and seeking to understand before responding. This approach not only prevents conflict but strengthens bonds by demonstrating respect and care.

The story of Nelson Mandela offers a powerful modern example of trust, empathy, and communication in action. Imprisoned for 27 years, Mandela could have emerged from captivity consumed by anger and bitterness. Instead, he chose reconciliation. His ability to empathize with his oppressors—to understand their fears and motivations—allowed him to bridge divides and heal a fractured nation. Mandela's relationships were built on trust earned through integrity, communication rooted in truth, and empathy that transcended personal pain. His life reminds us that even in the most difficult circumstances, connection is possible when we approach others with openness and compassion.

Building healthy relationships also requires boundaries—an often misunderstood aspect of connection. Boundaries are not barriers; they are expressions of self-respect that enable us to give freely without resentment. The Stoics, including Marcus Aurelius, understood the importance of recognizing what lies within our control and what does not. In relationships, this means accepting that we cannot change others; we can only choose how we respond. By setting clear boundaries—communicating our needs, honoring our values, and respecting our limits—we protect our emotional well-being while fostering healthier, more balanced connections.

Healthy relationships, then, are not passive; they are intentional. They require effort, humility, and a willingness to grow both individually and together. Marcus Aurelius teaches us that we cannot expect perfection from others or ourselves, but we can commit to showing up with integrity, empathy, and a spirit of collaboration. When we approach relationships as opportunities to learn, teach, and grow, we create bonds that withstand the tests of time and adversity.

In our fast-paced, often disconnected world, the wisdom of great minds reminds us of a timeless truth: connection is a choice. It is a choice to trust, to empathize, to communicate, and to forgive. It is a choice to see the humanity in others, to honor their struggles, and to share in their joys. By embodying these principles, we not only build stronger relationships but also contribute to a more compassionate and connected world—one bond at a time.

Love as a Unifying Force

In the most trying moments of human history, when communities fractured and nations seemed irreparably divided, a few individuals stood as beacons of hope, choosing love and compassion over hatred and violence. Figures such as Mahatma Gandhi, Mother Teresa, and Martin Luther King Jr. transformed love into a force capable of healing wounds, bridging divides, and restoring humanity's faith in itself. For them, love was not merely an emotion but a radical and actionable commitment—a deliberate choice to unite rather than divide. Their lives remind us that love, when channeled with purpose and conviction, possesses the power to reshape societies and redefine the human experience.

Gandhi, the leader of India's nonviolent independence movement, embodied love as both philosophy and practice. Drawing inspiration from Hindu principles and the teachings of Jesus Christ, Gandhi believed that *ahimsa*, or nonviolence, was inseparable from love. To resist violence, one must actively choose compassion and understanding—even toward one's oppressors. "Where there is love, there is life," he wrote, framing love as an antidote to hatred and destruction. Gandhi's nonviolent approach was not born of weakness but of extraordinary strength. It demanded patience, discipline, and a refusal to dehumanize others, no matter how justified anger might feel.

For Gandhi, love was a unifying force because it appealed to the humanity that exists in every individual. By refusing to retaliate against British oppression with violence, he demonstrated that love could disarm power and break cycles of hatred. His famous Salt March, where thousands of Indians peacefully protested the British salt tax, exemplified how collective action grounded in love could unite people across divides of caste, creed, and class. Gandhi understood that to build a free and just society, love had to transcend tribalism—it had to become a force that united rather than divided.

The relevance of Gandhi's teachings is profound in our modern world, where divisiveness often seems to dominate discourse. His example challenges us to resist the temptation of "us versus them" thinking and to seek common ground.

Love, Gandhi teaches us, is not passive—it is courageous and transformative. It requires us to see those we perceive as adversaries not as enemies but as fellow human beings who, like us, seek dignity, understanding, and peace.

Mother Teresa's mission, on the other hand, showcased love as a deeply personal and intimate force. While Gandhi sought to unite nations, Mother Teresa dedicated her life to healing individual suffering. Born in Albania and known for her work in the slums of Calcutta, Mother Teresa viewed every act of service—no matter how small—as an expression of love. "Not all of us can do great things," she famously said, "but we can do small things with great love." Her commitment to the poor, the sick, and the abandoned stemmed from her belief that love had the power to restore dignity to even the most overlooked and forgotten members of society.

Mother Teresa's work reminds us that love, at its core, is about seeing and honoring the humanity of others. In a world that often measures worth by status, wealth, or productivity, her example challenges us to love without conditions.

Whether offering food to the hungry, tending to the ill, or simply sitting with someone in their pain, Mother Teresa demonstrated that love's greatest strength lies in its simplicity. She saw love as an invitation to act—not just in grand gestures but in the everyday moments where kindness can make all the difference.

The lesson here is clear: love does not have to move mountains to be powerful. By showing compassion to those in our immediate circles— friends, family, colleagues, and strangers—we contribute to a larger current of unity and healing. It is in these small, intentional acts that love transforms the world.

While Gandhi and Mother Teresa worked in vastly different contexts, their message of love as a unifying force found a powerful echo in the life of Martin Luther King Jr. As the leader of the American Civil Rights Movement, King believed that love was the only force capable of dismantling hatred and oppression. Inspired by Gandhi's philosophy of nonviolence and the Christian ethic of love, King called for "agape"—a selfless, unconditional love that transcends personal feelings or biases. "Hate cannot drive out hate;

only love can do that," King declared, emphasizing that love had the power to heal both the
oppressed and the oppressor.

King's leadership during the Montgomery Bus
Boycott and the March on Washington illustrated the transformative potential of love in the
face of injustice. By refusing to meet violence
with violence, he and his followers exposed the
moral bankruptcy of segregation and awakened
the conscience of a nation. King's vision of the
"beloved community" — a society where love
and justice prevail — remains one of his most enduring legacies. He understood that true unity
required more than coexistence; it demanded
reconciliation, forgiveness, and a commitment
to shared dignity.

Today, King's call for love as a tool of unity is as
urgent as ever. In an era marked by polarization
and rising tensions, his life reminds us that love
is not weakness — it is strength. To choose love
in the face of hatred is a revolutionary act. It
requires us to listen when it is easier to shout, to
forgive when it is easier to resent, and to build
bridges when it is easier to burn them.

What unites Gandhi, Mother Teresa, and Martin Luther King Jr. is their unwavering belief that love has the power to transform individuals, communities, and entire societies. Their examples challenge us to reframe how we view love—not as mere sentimentality but as a force that requires action, sacrifice, and resolve. Love, they teach us, is the ultimate unifier because it sees beyond divisions. It reminds us that beneath our differences, we share a common humanity.

In our daily lives, we can embody this unifying love in both small and significant ways. It can mean extending understanding to someone with whom we disagree, offering kindness to a stranger, or working to heal wounds within our communities. Love does not erase conflict or hardship, but it provides a path forward—one that heals rather than harms, unites rather than divides.

By choosing love, we honor the wisdom of these visionaries who believed, against all odds, that humanity's greatest strength lies not in power or wealth but in our capacity to care for one another. Through love, we bridge divides, restore dignity, and create a world where connection and compassion triumph over division.

CHAPTER 2: THE ART OF HAPPINESS – INSIGHTS ON JOY AND CONTENTMENT

Philosophical Definitions of Happiness

For as long as humanity has pondered the meaning of life, it has sought to define happiness—the elusive state of joy, contentment, and fulfillment that seems as simple as it is complex. While happiness today is often pursued as a fleeting feeling, a rush brought on by external achievements or pleasures, the great minds of history viewed it as something far deeper. From Epicurus' gentle celebration of life's simple pleasures to the Stoics' unshakable pursuit of inner peace, happiness has always been seen as a matter of perspective, discipline, and virtue. Understanding these timeless definitions of happiness allows us to reconsider our own quest for joy, grounding it in principles that stand the test of time.

For Epicurus, the ancient Greek philosopher, happiness was found in simplicity. Living in Athens during the 4th century BCE, Epicurus believed that the pursuit of pleasure—the absence of pain—was the ultimate goal of human life. Yet this "pleasure" was often misunderstood, both in his time and ours. To Epicurus, true pleasure was not found in excess, indulgence, or wealth but in the quiet satisfaction of life's most basic and meaningful needs: friendship, freedom, and contemplation. In his *Letter to Menoeceus*, Epicurus wrote, "We must free ourselves from the prison of everyday affairs and politics, and seek peace of mind with like-minded friends."

Epicurus founded a small community known as "The Garden," where he and his followers cultivated a life free from unnecessary desires. Rather than striving for riches, fame, or luxury, they found joy in simple meals, laughter with close companions, and time spent in reflection. Epicurus taught that much of human unhappiness arises not from what we lack but from wanting too much. By learning to desire only what is essential, we can free ourselves from anxiety and discover a profound sense of contentment.

This wisdom remains strikingly relevant in the modern world. Today's culture, driven by consumerism and endless comparison, often ties happiness to the accumulation of wealth, status, or possessions. Yet Epicurus reminds us that the path to joy lies not in having more but in appreciating enough. To embrace his philosophy, we might pause and ask ourselves: What do I truly need to be happy? Often, the answer lies in what we already have—relationships, health, and moments of quiet connection with life itself. By simplifying our desires, we clear the noise of excess and make room for contentment.

In stark contrast to Epicurus' gentle pleasure, the Stoics—philosophers like Seneca, Epictetus, and Marcus Aurelius—viewed happiness as an internal state of peace achieved through acceptance of life's challenges. For the Stoics, the world was unpredictable, filled with trials, losses, and forces beyond human control. Yet rather than resisting these realities, the Stoics embraced them. They believed that happiness was not the absence of hardship but the ability to remain calm, resilient, and virtuous in its presence.

Seneca, the Roman statesman and Stoic philosopher, captured this beautifully when he wrote, "We suffer more in imagination than in reality." Much of our unhappiness, the Stoics argued, comes not from external events but from our reactions to them—our judgments, fears, and desires. By training ourselves to focus only on what lies within our control, we can cultivate a lasting sense of peace. This discipline of the mind, known as *ataraxia*, allowed the Stoics to maintain happiness regardless of external circumstances.

Epictetus, once a slave who became one of Rome's greatest teachers, illustrated this point with profound clarity. He taught that while we cannot control the actions of others, the weather, or fate itself, we can always control our own attitudes and responses. Happiness, therefore, is not something granted by fortune but something we create through perspective. "Man is not disturbed by events," Epictetus wrote, "but by the view he takes of them."

For modern readers, the Stoic view of happiness offers a practical antidote to life's inevitable challenges. In a world filled with uncertainty— career pressures, global crises, personal loss— the Stoic practice of acceptance and inner calm empowers us to navigate adversity without losing our peace of mind. It invites us to let go of the need for control and to focus instead on what we can change: our thoughts, our actions, and the virtues we embody. By choosing calm over chaos, we reclaim happiness as something unshakable and enduring.

The tension between Epicurean pleasure and Stoic acceptance reflects the diverse paths to happiness that have shaped human thought. While Epicurus invites us to savor life's simple joys, the Stoics challenge us to embrace life's storms with courage. Yet these two philosophies are not contradictory; they complement each other. Epicurus reminds us to slow down, to find joy in the present moment, while the Stoics remind us to persevere, to rise above the trials of life with dignity and grace. Together, they form a holistic approach to happiness—one that balances joy with resilience, simplicity with strength.

Both philosophies also share a common thread: the belief that happiness is an inside job. Whether through minimizing desires, as Epicurus taught, or mastering one's reactions, as the Stoics argued, happiness depends not on external circumstances but on the mind's ability to cultivate peace. This truth transcends time, offering us a powerful framework for navigating the complexities of modern life.

At its core, the search for happiness is a search for meaning—for a life that feels fulfilling, joyful, and authentic. The great philosophers teach us that happiness is not something we stumble upon but something we build, choice by choice. It is found not in the pursuit of pleasure or the avoidance of pain but in the ability to live intentionally, with awareness and gratitude for the present moment.

As we reflect on these timeless definitions, we might ask ourselves: What does happiness mean to me? Is it the joy of simple pleasures, the calm of inner peace, or the satisfaction of living a virtuous life? Perhaps it is all of these at once—a delicate balance that evolves as we do. The wisdom of Epicurus and the Stoics reminds us that happiness is always within reach, not as a distant destination but as a way of being. By simplifying our desires, mastering our perspectives, and living with intention, we unlock the art of happiness—one moment, one choice, one breath at a time.

The Role of Gratitude and Perspective

In the search for happiness, few tools are as simple yet transformative as gratitude and perspective. While many chase joy in achievements, possessions, or the future's promises, philosophers and thinkers remind us that happiness often lies in how we see what is already before us. Cicero, the great Roman statesman and philosopher, declared gratitude "the greatest of all virtues and the parent of all others." Modern psychology affirms this ancient wisdom, demonstrating that gratitude not only elevates mood but also shifts our focus from what we lack to the abundance already present in our lives. It is a reminder that joy is not found outside of us but within our capacity to perceive and appreciate the moment.

Cicero's emphasis on gratitude stems from his belief that it connects us to the essence of life itself. In his writings, he often spoke of gratitude as a practice that nourishes the soul and strengthens relationships. Gratitude, for Cicero, was not a passive emotion but an active recognition of life's gifts—be it the loyalty of a friend, the beauty of nature, or the simple pleasures of daily life. By consciously acknowledging the

good around us, Cicero believed, we elevate
our moral character and deepen our happiness.
Gratitude grounds us, pulling us out of restless-
ness and into the present moment.

This idea is strikingly relevant in today's fast-
paced world, where dissatisfaction is often fueled by comparison and a relentless pursuit of
"more." Social media, with its curated highlights
of other people's lives, can distort our perspectives, making us blind to our own blessings.
Here, Cicero's wisdom acts as a salve: By focusing on what we have rather than what we lack,
we reclaim contentment. Gratitude reframes our
perspective, teaching us to see life not as a series
of deficits but as a canvas of abundance.

Modern psychology provides scientific backing
for this ancient truth. Studies have shown that
cultivating gratitude rewires the brain, increas-
ing feelings of happiness and well-being. Dr.
Robert Emmons, one of the leading researchers
on gratitude, describes it as a two-step process:
first, we recognize the good in our lives; second,
we acknowledge that this goodness comes from
sources outside ourselves—whether it be other
people, nature, or fate itself. This act of recogni-

tion fosters humility and connection, reminding us of our place within a greater whole. Gratitude shifts our perspective outward, allowing us to see the world through a lens of appreciation rather than scarcity.

Consider the practice of keeping a gratitude journal, a simple exercise endorsed by modern thinkers and psychologists. By writing down three things we are grateful for each day—no matter how small—we train our minds to focus on the positive. A warm cup of coffee on a cold morning, a kind word from a stranger, the laughter of a child—these moments, when noticed and cherished, become sources of joy. The beauty of gratitude lies in its accessibility; it does not require wealth, status, or perfect circumstances. It requires only a willingness to look closely at the life we already have.

Perspective, too, plays a crucial role in our experience of happiness. How we interpret events, challenges, and even ordinary moments shapes our reality. The Stoics, including Seneca and Marcus Aurelius, believed that while we cannot control external circumstances, we can always control how we perceive them. Marcus Aurelius wrote, "The happiness of your life depends upon the quality of your thoughts." To the Stoics, perspective was power. It was the ability to reframe adversity as opportunity, to find silver linings in hardship, and to remain calm amidst the storms of life.

Viktor Frankl, the Austrian psychiatrist and Holocaust survivor, echoed this wisdom in his groundbreaking work *Man's Search for Meaning*. While enduring unimaginable suffering in Nazi concentration camps, Frankl discovered that perspective—the ability to find meaning in even the bleakest circumstances—was the key to survival. "Everything can be taken from a man but one thing: the last of the human freedoms—to choose one's attitude in any given set of circumstances," he wrote. Frankl's words are a testament to the resilience of the human spirit and the transformative power of perspective.

For readers navigating their own struggles, Frankl's lesson is clear: Happiness is not the absence of difficulty but the ability to shift one's perspective. By choosing to see challenges as opportunities for growth or to find beauty in imperfection, we reclaim our sense of agency.

Perspective teaches us that life is not always what happens to us but how we respond to it.

The interplay between gratitude and perspective becomes evident in the Japanese philosophy of *wabi-sabi*, which celebrates imperfection, impermanence, and the beauty of the ordinary. Rather than longing for an idealized version of life, *wabi-sabi* invites us to embrace life as it is— with all its flaws, cracks, and fleeting moments. A chipped teacup becomes beautiful because of its history; a fading sunset is cherished because it will not last. This mindset shifts our focus away from perfection and scarcity and toward appreciation for the present moment.

Incorporating gratitude and perspective into daily life is not a monumental task but a series of small, intentional choices. It can mean pausing to notice the sound of birds in the morning, savoring a meal shared with loved ones, or reflecting on the lessons learned from a difficult experience. These moments, when appreciated fully, weave joy into the fabric of our lives.

When Cicero called gratitude the "parent of all virtues," he understood its ripple effect. Grat-

itude fosters humility, connection, and generosity. Perspective, in turn, gives us the power
to shape our experience of the world. Together,
they offer a roadmap to happiness that is both
timeless and accessible. By cultivating gratitude
and shifting our perspective, we train ourselves
to see life through a lens of wonder and possibility.

The art of happiness, then, is not found in grand
achievements or perfect circumstances but in
our ability to notice, appreciate, and reframe.
In a world that often pulls our attention toward
what is missing, gratitude and perspective remind us of what is already enough. By choosing
to embrace these practices, we open ourselves to
joy—not as something distant or elusive but as
something present and alive in every moment
we take the time to see.

Living in Alignment with Values

Happiness is often portrayed as something external—a prize we chase or a state we stumble
upon when everything aligns perfectly. Yet history's greatest thinkers have consistently revealed a deeper truth: happiness emerges when

we live in harmony with our values. Socrates, the father of Western philosophy, and Viktor Frankl, the modern sage of existential resilience, understood that true contentment comes not from external circumstances but from an authentic life shaped by integrity, purpose, and alignment with what matters most. To know one's values and act in accordance with them is to unlock a form of happiness that neither fortune nor hardship can take away.

Socrates believed that the unexamined life was not worth living. For him, the pursuit of truth and virtue was the key to a meaningful existence. Unlike his contemporaries, who defined happiness through wealth, pleasure, or power, Socrates argued that a life devoted to external rewards would inevitably leave us empty. True happiness, he insisted, arises from a life of moral integrity—a life in which one's actions reflect one's deepest principles. "Let him who would move the world first move himself," he proclaimed, urging individuals to turn inward, to question their beliefs, and to align their behavior with their values.

Socrates' method of questioning—what we now

call the Socratic method — was designed to strip away illusions and reveal truth. He challenged Athenians to ask themselves uncomfortable questions: What is good? What is just? What kind of life is worth living? By seeking these answers, Socrates believed, individuals could define their values and begin living with purpose. His insistence on authenticity was so strong that it cost him his life; sentenced to death for corrupting the youth of Athens, Socrates refused to compromise his principles. In his final moments, he remained true to his values, choosing integrity over survival.

The lesson Socrates offers is clear: happiness is inseparable from authenticity. To live in alignment with our values is to live without regret, without the quiet burden of knowing we have betrayed ourselves. In a modern world filled with distractions and pressures to conform, Socrates' call to examine our lives feels more urgent than ever. Are we living for what truly matters, or are we chasing goals imposed upon us by society, family, or culture? Socrates reminds us that happiness begins with clarity — clarity about what we believe, what we value, and who we choose to become.

Viktor Frankl, writing two millennia after Socrates, arrived at a similar truth through vastly different circumstances. A psychiatrist and Holocaust survivor, Frankl endured unimaginable suffering in Nazi concentration camps. Yet, even in the face of starvation, dehumanization, and death, Frankl discovered a profound insight: happiness and meaning are found not in external circumstances but in our response to them. "Everything can be taken from a man but one thing: the last of the human freedoms—to choose one's attitude in any given set of circumstances, to choose one's own way," he wrote.

For Frankl, this freedom of choice was the gateway to a meaningful life. While imprisoned, he observed that those who survived were not necessarily the physically strongest but those who had a clear sense of purpose—a reason to endure. Frankl himself found meaning in his love for his wife, in the dream of publishing his work, and in the small moments of dignity he could preserve. He understood that even in the bleakest conditions, one could choose to act in alignment with one's values: to show kindness, to offer hope, to remain human.

Frankl's philosophy, which he later called *logo-therapy*, teaches that happiness arises when we align our actions with our purpose. Unlike fleeting pleasures or external success, meaning is durable; it sustains us through life's inevitable challenges. Frankl's wisdom resonates deeply with the modern reader. In an era where busyness is mistaken for purpose and distractions abound, we risk drifting through life without asking: What truly matters to me? What am I living for? Like Socrates, Frankl invites us to clarify our values and commit to living them fully.

Living in alignment with one's values requires both introspection and courage. It begins with self-awareness—the willingness to pause and reflect on what gives our lives meaning. For some, this might involve the pursuit of knowledge or creativity; for others, it may be the love shared with family or the desire to serve others. Whatever form our values take, they act as a compass, guiding us through both calm waters and storms. When life challenges us, values provide stability. They remind us who we are and what we stand for, even when the world feels chaotic.

Practical applications of this wisdom are surprisingly simple but profoundly transformative. Take the act of identifying core values—principles such as honesty, compassion, or growth. Writing them down and reflecting on them regularly can help us navigate difficult decisions. For instance, when faced with a moral dilemma at work or a strained relationship, asking "Does this action reflect my values?" can provide clarity and confidence. Living authentically may not always be easy—it often requires sacrifice, vulnerability, and discomfort—but it yields a deep sense of fulfillment that cannot be found in compromise.

Consider the story of Nelson Mandela, who spent 27 years imprisoned for his resistance to apartheid in South Africa. Like Socrates and Frankl, Mandela refused to betray his values, even when his freedom and life were at stake. Upon his release, Mandela chose forgiveness over vengeance, uniting a divided nation through the strength of his moral clarity. Mandela's life illustrates that living in alignment with values is not just a path to personal happiness but a force capable of transforming the world.

In our daily lives, the choice to live authentically may not always feel heroic, but it is no
less significant. It can mean speaking up when
silence feels safer, pursuing a passion when
others doubt us, or prioritizing relationships
over success. Each time we honor our values, we
strengthen our sense of self and contribute to a
life rich with meaning.

Socrates, Viktor Frankl, and modern examples
like Mandela remind us that happiness is not
found in perfection or ease but in the courage
to live truthfully. When our actions align with
our values, we create a life that feels whole,
consistent, and free of regret. We may still face
hardships, but with clarity of purpose, we endure them with grace. In the words of Frankl,
"Those who have a 'why' to live can bear almost
any 'how.'"

Ultimately, the art of happiness lies in the
choices we make each day. By defining what
we value, embracing authenticity, and acting
with purpose, we cultivate a life that is not only
joyful but meaningful. In aligning our actions

with our values, we find not just happiness but the profound satisfaction of a life well lived.

Inner Peace in a Chaotic World

In a world that often feels relentless—its noise unceasing, its demands overwhelming—finding peace can seem like an impossible pursuit. The pressures of modern life, with its chaotic blend of responsibilities, expectations, and uncertainties, pull us in countless directions. Yet the ancient wisdom of Eastern philosophies like Buddhism and Taoism offers a profound reminder: true peace does not come from the world around us but from within. Contentment, they teach us, arises when we let go of attachment, embrace the present moment, and cultivate harmony with the flow of life itself. Inner peace, therefore, is not an escape from the chaos of the world but a state of mind that remains steady within it.

The teachings of the Buddha are perhaps the most enduring exploration of this idea. Born in India in the 6th century BCE, Siddhartha Gautama—the Buddha—observed that human suffering arises from our attachment to desires, expectations, and outcomes. We chase pleasure, cling to what we cannot keep, and resist the inevitable changes of life. This endless grasping, he taught, creates turmoil within us, leaving us restless and discontent. "Peace comes from within," the Buddha said. "Do not seek it without." The path to inner peace lies not in controlling the world but in changing how we relate to it.

At the heart of Buddhist teachings is the practice of *mindfulness*—a deep, intentional awareness of the present moment. Mindfulness is the antidote to distraction, anxiety, and overthinking; it grounds us in the "now," where peace can be found regardless of external circumstances. Whether through meditation, breath awareness, or simply observing life without judgment, mindfulness invites us to slow down and notice the beauty and stillness available in each moment. When we stop resisting what is—when we accept reality as it is—we create space for calm to take root.

Consider the story of the stormy lake, often used as a metaphor in Buddhist teachings. When a lake is agitated, its surface becomes chaotic, and its depths remain unseen. But when the wind subsides, the water stills, and clarity is restored. Our minds, too, are like this lake. The chaos of life may stir our thoughts, creating ripples of worry, fear, and frustration. Yet through mindfulness, we can quiet the winds and find stillness. Beneath the turbulence, peace is always present, waiting to be discovered.

Taoism, the ancient Chinese philosophy rooted in the teachings of Lao Tzu, offers a similar but complementary vision of inner peace. In his seminal text, the *Tao Te Ching*, Lao Tzu describes the *Tao*—the natural flow of life—as the source of harmony and contentment. To live in alignment with the Tao is to surrender to the rhythms of existence, trusting in life's unfolding without force or resistance. "When you realize there is nothing lacking," Lao Tzu wrote, "the whole world belongs to you."

Central to Taoist thought is the concept of *wu wei*, often translated as "non-action" or "effortless action." It does not mean passivity but rather acting in harmony with the natural order, allowing life to flow without unnecessary struggle. Imagine a river winding its way through a landscape. It does not resist the rocks or hills in its path; it flows around them, adapting with ease. In the same way, Taoism teaches us to let go of the need to control or force outcomes. By accepting life's ebbs and flows, we discover that peace is found not in fighting the current but in moving with it.

This philosophy holds particular relevance in our modern lives, where the drive for control often leaves us exhausted and disillusioned. We plan, predict, and prepare, only to find that life refuses to conform to our expectations. Here, Taoist wisdom offers freedom: by surrendering to uncertainty and trusting the process, we release the anxiety that arises from resistance. To practice *wu wei* is to understand that peace comes not from forcing the world to meet our desires but from aligning ourselves with the world as it is.

Mindfulness and Taoist acceptance are not abstract ideals; they are practices that can be integrated into everyday life. When we feel overwhelmed, simply pausing to observe the breath can anchor us in the present moment. Each inhale and exhale becomes a reminder that we are alive, here, and now. Similarly, embracing *wu wei* might mean approaching challenges with flexibility, asking, "How can I adapt to this moment?" rather than fighting against it.

The poet and Zen practitioner Thich Nhat Hanh, a modern embodiment of Buddhist mindfulness, offered practical guidance for finding peace amidst chaos. He taught that even the simplest activities—drinking tea, walking, or washing dishes—could become opportunities for mindfulness. "Peace is every step," he wrote, reminding us that tranquility is not a distant destination but something we create with our awareness in each moment. By focusing fully on the task at hand, we quiet the mind's chatter and discover a deep, quiet joy.

This approach is especially valuable in today's world, where technology and busyness often fragment our attention. We scroll through screens while eating meals, plan the future while walking outside, and multitask endlessly. Yet mindfulness calls us back to the present, where life is actually happening. It invites us to savor small moments—a sip of water, the feel of sunlight on our skin, the sound of laughter— moments we often miss in our rush to the next thing.

Inner peace, then, is not the absence of chaos but the ability to remain centered within it. The Buddha's mindfulness and Lao Tzu's surrender teach us that we cannot always control life's storms, but we can choose how we respond. We can meet challenges with acceptance, observe the present without judgment, and trust that peace lies not in fixing the world but in stilling the mind.

In the end, finding contentment in a chaotic world requires a shift in perspective—a recognition that peace is not something we chase but something we allow. Like the calm beneath the stormy lake, it is already within us, waiting to be uncovered. The practices of mindfulness, acceptance, and surrender guide us back to this truth, offering a path to happiness that transcends circumstances. By learning to be present, to flow with life, and to let go of what we cannot control, we cultivate an unshakable peace—one that endures regardless of what the world may bring.

CHAPTER 3:
FINDING PURPOSE
– THE SEARCH FOR
MEANING IN LIFE

The Eternal Quest for Meaning

The search for meaning is one of humanity's oldest and most profound pursuits. Across cultures and eras, the question "Why am I here?" has echoed in the hearts of individuals, driving them to explore life's purpose. This eternal quest transcends religion, philosophy, and science; it is a fundamental yearning that binds us all. From Friedrich Nietzsche's defiant call for self-creation to Søren Kierkegaard's embrace of faith in the face of uncertainty, and Lao Tzu's wisdom on living in harmony with the flow of existence, the search for meaning lies at the core of what it means to be human.

Nietzsche, the 19th-century German philosopher, famously declared, "He who has a why to live can bear almost any how." His work often confronted life's inherent difficulties and chaos, yet rather than despair, Nietzsche urged individuals to create their own meaning. In a world where traditional structures—religion, morality, and authority—seemed to crumble, Nietzsche called on humanity to transcend these systems and define its own purpose. He introduced the concept of the *Übermensch*, or "overman," an individual who rises above societal norms to create a life of self-determined meaning.

For Nietzsche, purpose was not something discovered but something forged. He rejected passivity and challenged individuals to take responsibility for their existence, to transform suffering and uncertainty into growth. "To live is to suffer, to survive is to find some meaning in the suffering," he wrote, framing purpose as a choice—a decision to imbue life with significance through courage, creativity, and authenticity. His philosophy resonates deeply with modern readers, who often face the same existential void that Nietzsche described. When confronted with a world that feels chaotic or meaningless, his call to create purpose offers a path forward: we are not passive observers of our lives; we are the authors.

Søren Kierkegaard, the Danish philosopher and father of existentialism, approached the search for meaning through a different lens—one of faith, humility, and personal responsibility. Kierkegaard believed that life's greatest challenge was not discovering universal truths but embracing the subjective, individual journey toward meaning. He emphasized the importance of confronting life's uncertainty and limitations rather than escaping them. For Kierkegaard, this confrontation often required a "leap of faith" — a conscious decision to trust in something greater than oneself, even when clarity is absent.

In his work *Fear and Trembling*, Kierkegaard reflected on the biblical story of Abraham, who was asked to sacrifice his son Isaac as an act of obedience to God. To Kierkegaard, Abraham's willingness to act despite his fear and confusion exemplified the essence of faith: a commitment to meaning in the face of doubt. This leap of faith, Kierkegaard argued, was not irrational but deeply human. It allowed individuals to transcend despair and find purpose, even when life's answers seemed elusive.

Kierkegaard's message speaks to modern readers navigating a world that offers endless distractions yet little direction. His philosophy challenges us to engage fully with life's uncertainties, to resist the temptation of apathy, and to trust that purpose is not always something we see clearly — it is something we commit to, step by step. For those who feel lost or overwhelmed, Kierkegaard's leap of faith is a powerful reminder: meaning is not found in perfect clarity but in the act of believing, choosing, and persevering.

While Nietzsche and Kierkegaard wrestled with the individual's relationship to meaning, Lao Tzu, the ancient Chinese philosopher and founder of Taoism, offered a vision of purpose rooted in harmony with the natural world. In the *Tao Te Ching*, Lao Tzu described the *Tao*—the underlying way or flow of life—as the source of all meaning. Unlike Western thinkers who emphasized struggle and creation, Lao Tzu taught that meaning arises when we surrender to the rhythms of existence and align ourselves with the natural order.

"To the mind that is still," Lao Tzu wrote, "the whole universe surrenders." This stillness—a quiet acceptance of what is—forms the essence of Taoist wisdom. Rather than forcing purpose onto life, Lao Tzu invites us to observe, listen, and flow with life's unfolding. He describes the concept of *wu wei*, or "effortless action," as the path to meaning. Like a river that adapts to obstacles by flowing around them, we find purpose not through resistance but through ease, simplicity, and presence.

Lao Tzu's teachings challenge the modern obsession with control and achievement. In our relentless pursuit of success, we often overlook life's deeper meaning—the beauty of the present moment, the interconnectedness of all things, and the peace that comes from surrendering to what we cannot change. Purpose, according to Lao Tzu, is not something grand or external; it is found in living authentically, harmoniously, and with awareness.

Together, the philosophies of Nietzsche, Kierkegaard, and Lao Tzu offer a powerful framework for understanding the search for meaning. Nietzsche's call to create purpose teaches us to take ownership of our lives, to transform suffering into growth. Kierkegaard's leap of faith reminds us that meaning often requires courage and commitment, even in uncertainty. Lao Tzu's vision of harmony shows us that purpose can be found not through struggle but through stillness and alignment.

In practical terms, these insights offer guidance for navigating our own search for meaning. When life feels chaotic or directionless, Nietzsche urges us to ask: What can I create from this? How can I shape this experience into something meaningful? Kierkegaard challenges us to embrace uncertainty with faith, to trust that our choices matter even when clarity is absent. Lao Tzu reminds us to slow down, to observe life's flow, and to find purpose in the simplicity of being.

Ultimately, the search for meaning is not a single revelation but a lifelong journey—a process of discovery, creation, and alignment. It is a quest that invites us to reflect deeply on who we are, what we value, and how we choose to live. The great minds remind us that meaning is not given; it is chosen. It is forged in the way we rise to challenges, embrace uncertainties, and remain present to life's unfolding beauty.

The eternal quest for meaning is what makes us human. It drives us to seek, to question, and to strive for something beyond ourselves. Whether through creation, faith, or harmony, we find purpose not in answers but in the act of searching. It is in this search that life becomes rich with significance, revealing that the journey itself is the meaning we seek.

Aligning Purpose with Action

To have a sense of purpose without action is like owning a compass but refusing to move. Purpose, at its core, is dynamic. It is not simply an idea or an abstract longing; it is something realized through effort, through movement, and through our responses to life's circumstances. This connection between purpose and action—particularly in times of hardship—is the foundation of Viktor Frankl's teachings and the existentialist thinkers who followed him. They understood that meaning is not found passively but created actively, often in the face of struggle. It is through action that purpose transforms from an intangible dream into a living, breathing reality.

Viktor Frankl, the Austrian psychiatrist and Holocaust survivor, witnessed firsthand humanity's potential to create purpose even in unimaginable suffering. In the Nazi concentration camps, stripped of all possessions and faced with brutal dehumanization, Frankl discovered that survival often depended not on physical strength but on the ability to find meaning amidst despair. In his seminal work, *Man's Search for Meaning*, Frankl wrote, "Life is never made unbearable by circumstances, but only by lack of meaning and purpose." He saw that even in the darkest moments, individuals who could identify a purpose—whether it was the hope of reuniting with a loved one, the completion of unfinished work, or the simple determination to retain their dignity—were able to endure suffering with a strength that defied their circumstances.

Frankl's experiences shaped his theory of *logotherapy*, which posits that humans are motivated by a "will to meaning"—a drive to find purpose even in the face of suffering. Unlike the pursuit of pleasure, which can be fleeting, or the drive for power, which can be corrosive, the will to meaning is enduring. It gives life structure and direction, particularly when external comforts fail. Frankl urged individuals to take responsibility for their existence, arguing that meaning is not something we stumble upon; it is something we create through action. He asked, "What is life expecting of me?" rather than "What do I expect of life?" In doing so, he reframed purpose as a call to respond to challenges with courage, integrity, and intention.

This lesson is deeply relevant in a world that often feels unmoored. When we are faced with personal loss, professional setbacks, or moments of uncertainty, Frankl's wisdom challenges us to ask: How can I respond to this? What can I create from this struggle? Rather than being paralyzed by hardship, we are invited to act—to take small, meaningful steps that align with our values and contribute to a larger purpose. In choosing our response, we regain agency, even when circumstances are beyond our control.

Existentialist thinkers, such as Jean-Paul Sartre and Simone de Beauvoir, echoed Frankl's emphasis on action as the pathway to purpose. Sartre, in particular, argued that life has no inherent meaning; instead, it is up to each individual to create their own through their choices and actions. This freedom, Sartre noted, is both liberating and terrifying. It places responsibility squarely in our hands, requiring us to define what matters most and act accordingly. "Man is nothing else but what he makes of himself,"

Sartre famously wrote. Purpose, in his view, is an ongoing project—something we construct day by day, through the decisions we make and the lives we choose to lead.

For Sartre, action was a declaration of existence. To act with purpose was to affirm one's identity and embrace life's possibilities, no matter how uncertain or limited they might seem. Passivity, on the other hand, was a form of self-betrayal—a refusal to engage fully with life's challenges and opportunities. In this way, Sartre's philosophy reminds us that purpose requires courage. It asks us to take risks, to step into the unknown, and to actively shape our own narrative.

Simone de Beauvoir extended this idea to the realm of relationships and societal engagement, emphasizing that purpose is not just an individual endeavor but one that connects us to others. For de Beauvoir, meaningful action often involves contributing to the freedom and well-being of others. "In helping others, I make something of myself," she wrote, illustrating how purpose can be amplified when we act in service of something greater than ourselves. Whether through personal relationships, creative work, or acts of kindness, our actions ripple outward, creating meaning not just for ourselves but for the world around us.

Practical applications of these philosophies can be found in the lives of countless individuals who have turned hardship into purpose. Consider Malala Yousafzai, who, after surviving an attack by the Taliban, chose to dedicate her life to advocating for girls' education. Her response to suffering was not despair or passivity but action rooted in purpose—a purpose that continues to inspire millions. Malala's story reflects Frankl's idea that meaning can arise from the very struggles that threaten to break us. Rather than being defined by hardship, she used it as fuel to align her actions with her deepest values.

In our own lives, aligning purpose with action does not require grand gestures or extraordinary circumstances. It begins with small, intentional choices. It means showing up for what matters—whether that is pursuing meaningful work, strengthening relationships, or contributing to causes that align with our values. Purpose, after all, is not static; it evolves as we do. By taking action, even in the face of uncertainty or difficulty, we give our lives direction and momentum. We transform purpose from a distant ideal into something tangible and alive.

The connection between purpose and action also offers a powerful antidote to inertia. In moments when we feel lost, overwhelmed, or unmotivated, it is easy to believe that purpose will find us—that clarity will arrive before we take the first step. Yet Frankl and the existentialists remind us that action often precedes meaning. Purpose does not always reveal itself in advance; it emerges as we engage with life, experiment, and persevere. The simple act of moving forward—of choosing one meaningful action in the present—can spark the sense of purpose we seek.

Ultimately, aligning purpose with action requires us to take ownership of our lives. It challenges us to ask, as Frankl did, "What is life expecting of me?" and to respond with courage and integrity. Whether through small daily choices or significant acts of resilience, we create meaning not by avoiding struggle but by engaging with it fully. The existentialists remind us that we are the architects of our purpose; the power lies within us to shape our lives in ways that are meaningful, authentic, and true.

In this alignment of purpose and action, life becomes rich with significance. The struggles we endure are no longer meaningless; they become opportunities to create, to grow, and to contribute. As Frankl so powerfully demonstrated, purpose is not something we wait for—it is something we do. It is found not in the absence of hardship but in our response to it, in the way we rise each day and choose to live with intention.

Contribution and Service to Others

A life driven by purpose is rarely lived in isolation. At the heart of a meaningful existence lies a profound truth: when we serve others, we create purpose not just for ourselves but for the world around us. The teachings of great leaders like Aristotle and the Dalai Lama illuminate this connection, showing us that contribution—to our families, communities, and humanity at large—can be a wellspring of deep, enduring fulfillment. Living a life of service shifts our focus outward, transforming individual purpose into something larger, something that leaves a lasting mark on the world.

Aristotle, the ancient Greek philosopher, believed that humans are social beings, intrinsically tied to one another. In his *Nicomachean Ethics*, Aristotle explored the concept of *eudaimonia*—a flourishing life—and identified virtue as the means to achieve it. To Aristotle, true happiness was not found in pleasure or wealth but in living virtuously and contributing to the greater good of society. He argued that purpose is realized through acts that honor our shared humanity. "What is the essence of life?" he asked. "To serve others and to do good."

For Aristotle, contributing to others was not simply a moral obligation; it was a path to personal fulfillment. By helping others thrive, we cultivate virtues such as kindness, generosity, and justice, which enrich our character and align us with our highest selves. He viewed service not as self-sacrifice but as self-expression—the natural outcome of living in accordance with our values and recognizing our interdependence. In Aristotle's vision, a life of service benefits not just society but the individual, who experiences happiness as a result of living meaningfully.

This philosophy remains deeply relevant in a modern world where isolation and disconnection are increasingly common. Many people pursue purpose through personal success or achievement but find themselves unfulfilled, as these pursuits often lack a connection to something greater. Aristotle reminds us that meaning is amplified when it transcends the self. By contributing to others—whether through acts of kindness, mentorship, or service—we find purpose in relationships, shared goals, and collective well-being.

The Dalai Lama, the spiritual leader of Tibetan Buddhism, extends Aristotle's insights by framing service as an expression of compassion. For the Dalai Lama, compassion—the ability to recognize and respond to the suffering of others—is at the heart of a purposeful life. "If you want others to be happy, practice compassion," he says. "If you want to be happy, practice compassion." This wisdom reflects a profound truth: in helping others, we help ourselves. Service creates a sense of connection, dissolves feelings of loneliness, and reminds us of our shared humanity.

The Dalai Lama's teachings emphasize that acts of service do not have to be grand or extraordinary to create meaning. He encourages us to approach every interaction with kindness, to offer help when we can, and to cultivate a spirit of generosity. Whether it is a smile, a listening ear, or a helping hand, small acts of compassion ripple outward, creating positive change in ways we may never fully see. In serving others, we move beyond the boundaries of our own struggles and experience the joy that comes from making a difference.

These lessons are exemplified in the lives of individuals who have dedicated themselves to serving others. Consider Mother Teresa, whose work with the poor and sick in Calcutta became a testament to the power of compassion. She once said, "Not all of us can do great things. But we can do small things with great love." Her life reminds us that purpose is not reserved for those who achieve extraordinary fame or recognition. It is found in the quiet, consistent acts of service that uplift others and honor the dignity of all people.

Modern research supports what Aristotle, the
Dalai Lama, and Mother Teresa intuitively understood: serving others creates a deep sense of
fulfillment. Studies have shown that individuals
who engage in acts of kindness or contribute
to their communities report higher levels of
happiness, reduced stress, and greater overall
well-being. This phenomenon, known as the
"helper's high," reflects the biological and emotional benefits of service. When we help others,
our brains release endorphins, creating a sense
of joy and connection. The act of giving, it seems,
is as rewarding as it is meaningful.

The challenge for many is finding ways to contribute amidst the busyness of modern life. It is
easy to believe that service requires significant
time, resources, or sacrifice, but this is not the
case. As the Dalai Lama teaches, acts of service begin with intention—with choosing to
approach life with compassion and awareness.
Contribution can take countless forms: volun-
teering for a cause we care about, supporting a
friend through a difficult time, sharing knowledge or skills, or simply offering a moment of
kindness to a stranger. The size of the act mat-

ters far less than the intention behind it.

In our professional lives, aligning our work with a sense of contribution can transform the way we experience purpose. Aristotle believed that work was not merely a means of survival but an opportunity to express our values and serve others. Whether we are teachers, healthcare workers, artists, or entrepreneurs, our efforts become meaningful when they contribute to something greater—when they solve problems, inspire others, or create beauty in the world. By asking, "Who does my work serve?" we shift our focus from personal gain to collective impact.

For those seeking purpose, the act of contributing to others offers clarity and direction. When we feel uncertain about our path, service can become a guiding light, reminding us of what truly matters. In helping others, we reconnect with our own humanity and discover a deeper sense of belonging. This is the paradox of purpose: when we give, we receive. When we focus on others, we find ourselves.

Ultimately, the teachings of Aristotle and the

Dalai Lama converge on a single truth: a life of purpose is a life lived for others. Contribution transforms individual meaning into something greater—something that echoes beyond our own existence. Whether through compassion, service, or acts of kindness, we create a legacy of impact that endures. In serving others, we fulfill not only their needs but also our own deepest longing: to live a life that matters.

In the end, purpose is not found in isolation but in connection. It is found in the moments when we choose to lift others, to offer compassion, and to make the world just a little bit better. By living a life of contribution, we honor the wisdom of the great minds who came before us and fulfill the timeless truth they taught: in serving others, we discover the purpose that makes life truly meaningful.

Small Moments, Big Purpose

When we imagine purpose, we often picture extraordinary acts: leaders who change the course of history, heroes who save lives, or creators who leave behind timeless masterpieces. These grand achievements, while inspiring, can make purpose seem distant—something reserved for the extraordinary few. Yet ancient wisdom and contemporary insights remind us of a simple truth: purpose is not always found in sweeping gestures. Often, it is in life's smallest moments—those unassuming, everyday acts—that meaning reveals itself. A quiet conversation, a moment of kindness, a mindful pause—these moments, seemingly insignificant, ripple outward in ways that can transform lives, including our own.

The 20th-century Japanese philosophy of *ikigai* embodies this concept beautifully. Translated loosely as "reason for being," *ikigai* describes purpose as something embedded in the ordinary rhythms of life. It is found in the small, meaningful actions that give us joy, connect us to others, and align us with the present moment. For some, *ikigai* may be the satisfaction of preparing a meal for loved ones; for others, it may be found in tending a garden, solving a problem at work, or offering a comforting word to a friend. Unlike grand notions of success, *ikigai* teaches us that purpose is not about scale—it is about depth. It is about fully engaging with what we do and recognizing the beauty in the everyday.

This wisdom echoes through the words of Mother Teresa, whose life exemplified the power of small acts. "Not all of us can do great things," she said, "but we can do small things with great love." For Mother Teresa, purpose was found not in fame or recognition but in the moments of service that brought comfort to others. Holding a hand, offering a smile, or speaking a word of encouragement—these simple gestures, repeated daily, became profound expressions of purpose. Her life reminds us that it is not the size of our actions that matters but the intention and love we bring to them.

Similarly, the Buddhist concept of mindfulness offers a path to finding purpose in the small moments of everyday life. Thich Nhat Hanh, the renowned Zen teacher, described mindfulness as the art of being fully present. "Drink your tea slowly and reverently, as if it is the axis on which the world earth revolves," he wrote, capturing the essence of mindfulness as an appreciation for life's smallest gifts. By engaging fully with simple activities—eating, walking, breathing—we cultivate a sense of purpose that transcends busyness and distraction. These moments, when lived with awareness, become meaningful because they connect us to the present and remind us of life's inherent beauty.

In our fast-paced modern world, where success is often measured in productivity or acclaim, this perspective can be revolutionary. It challenges us to slow down and notice the purpose embedded in our daily routines. A teacher helping a child grasp a difficult concept, a barista offering a warm smile to a hurried customer, or a parent reading a bedtime story—all these moments contain quiet purpose. They may seem small, but they contribute to the well-being of others and reflect values of care, connection, and service.

Viktor Frankl, who so profoundly explored meaning in his work *Man's Search for Meaning*, also recognized the significance of small acts in a life of purpose. For Frankl, meaning was not reserved for monumental achievements but was often found in the mundane. In the concentration camps where he endured unimaginable suffering, Frankl observed that small, everyday choices—offering comfort to a fellow prisoner,

sharing a piece of bread, or maintaining a sense
of dignity—became acts of profound purpose.
He believed that even the smallest moments
could reveal life's meaning when approached
with intention.

Frankl's insight speaks directly to those who
feel their lives lack purpose because they do not
achieve grand feats. He reminds us that purpose
is not about scale; it is about presence. A single
moment of kindness, courage, or connection can
carry as much meaning as the loftiest achievement. Purpose, Frankl believed, is accessible to
everyone because it is not something external—
it is something we bring to the world through
our choices, no matter how small.

The Japanese tradition of *kintsugi*, or "golden
joinery," offers a fitting metaphor for this idea.
In *kintsugi*, broken pottery is repaired with lac-
quer mixed with gold, highlighting the cracks
rather than hiding them. The result is a piece
that is more beautiful and unique for having
been broken. This philosophy teaches us to find
beauty and purpose in imperfection and small,
seemingly insignificant moments. Just as the
cracks are celebrated, our lives are enriched by

the small moments that give them texture and meaning.

Practically, this wisdom invites us to reframe how we view our daily lives. Rather than waiting for a grand calling, we can look for opportunities to bring purpose into the present moment. A phone call to check on a friend, a kind word to a stranger, or the effort we put into our work—these small actions add up to a life of meaning. Purpose does not require us to do something extraordinary; it asks only that we approach the ordinary with intention, care, and presence.

Consider the story of Fred Rogers, better known as "Mister Rogers," who embodied this philosophy through his decades of work in children's television. Rogers believed that every interaction, no matter how small, was an opportunity to make a difference. His gentle, thoughtful conversations with children, filled with kindness and understanding, shaped generations. Rogers' legacy was not built on grand gestures but on his unwavering commitment to treating each moment—and each person—as meaningful. His life reminds us that purpose is not something we achieve; it is something we practice, one small act at a time.

In the end, purpose is not found in waiting for monumental moments to arrive but in showing up fully for the life we already have. It is in the way we care for those around us, the way we honor our values through small choices, and the way we embrace each moment as an opportunity to connect, contribute, and grow. The wisdom of Mother Teresa, Thich Nhat Hanh, and Viktor Frankl invites us to see the beauty and significance in the ordinary.

When we pause to recognize the purpose in small moments, life takes on new meaning. Each interaction, each act of kindness, each mindful breath becomes a thread in the larger tapestry of a meaningful life. In this way, purpose is not something distant or unattainable—it is right here, waiting for us in the quiet, beautiful moments that make up our days. By choosing to live with intention and presence, we discover that even the smallest acts can hold the greatest purpose.

CHAPTER 4: RESILIENCE OF THE HUMAN SPIRIT – LESSONS ON OVERCOMING ADVERSITY

The Philosophy of Suffering and Growth

To live is to face suffering, a truth that stretches across cultures, generations, and belief systems. While hardship is a shared human experience, our response to it determines whether we are broken by suffering or transformed through it. The Stoics—thinkers like Seneca and Marcus Aurelius—understood this reality better than most. For them, suffering was not merely something to endure but a teacher, a crucible that shapes character and reveals inner strength. By accepting adversity and viewing it as an opportunity for growth, they uncovered a timeless truth: it is through struggle that the human spirit becomes resilient and refined.

Seneca, the Roman statesman and Stoic philosopher, explored the nature of suffering extensively in his writings. Living in an era of political instability, betrayal, and personal loss, Seneca was no stranger to hardship. Yet rather than lamenting his struggles, he reframed them as opportunities for self-improvement. "Difficulties strengthen the mind, as labor does the body," he wrote, arguing that adversity is a necessary condition for growth. Just as a muscle must experience strain to become stronger, the human spirit must be tested to develop resilience, wisdom, and grace.

Seneca saw suffering not as a punishment but as a training ground. To him, life's challenges provided a chance to cultivate virtues like patience, courage, and fortitude. "A gem cannot be polished without friction, nor a man perfected without trials," he observed, urging us to view hardship as part of the process of becoming our best selves. For modern readers, this wisdom serves as a powerful reminder: growth does not happen in comfort. It happens when we are stretched beyond our limits, forced to confront pain, and ultimately rise stronger because of it.

Marcus Aurelius, the Roman Emperor and fellow Stoic, expanded on these ideas in his personal journal, *Meditations*. Written as reflections to himself during times of war, illness, and loss, Marcus Aurelius' words reveal a leader who viewed suffering as a path to inner fortitude. "The impediment to action advances action," he wrote. "What stands in the way becomes the way." This phrase encapsulates the essence of Stoic resilience: obstacles are not barriers but opportunities. Hardship, when approached with the right mindset, becomes the very thing that propels us forward.

To Marcus Aurelius, the key to enduring suffering lay in acceptance—what the Stoics called *amor fati*, or "love of fate." Rather than resisting what we cannot control, he believed we should embrace it. "You have power over your mind—not outside events," he reflected. "Realize this, and you will find strength." For Marcus Aurelius, suffering was not defined by the event itself but by our perception of it. By choosing to see challenges as opportunities for growth, we reclaim agency and find meaning even in the face of adversity.

The wisdom of Seneca and Marcus Aurelius resonates deeply in today's world, where hardship often feels overwhelming and senseless. Their philosophy offers a practical framework for navigating suffering with grace. First, they teach us to accept adversity as an inevitable part of life. To resist suffering is to amplify its pain, but to embrace it is to transform it. Second, they remind us that suffering is not a reflection of our weakness but an opportunity to cultivate strength. Each challenge we face becomes a chance to grow, to refine our character, and to uncover reserves of resilience we may not have known existed.

This perspective finds echoes in modern psychology, particularly in the concept of *post-traumatic growth*. Researchers have found that individuals who endure significant hardships often emerge with a renewed sense of purpose, deeper appreciation for life, and greater emotional strength. Just as the Stoics observed, it is not the suffering itself that defines us but how we respond to it. By choosing to view hardship as a teacher, we can reframe our struggles as pathways to growth rather than barriers to happiness.

Consider the story of a craftsman working with iron. To forge a strong and beautiful sword, the metal must be heated, hammered, and shaped repeatedly. Without the fire, the iron remains unrefined; without the blows, it cannot take form. In the same way, suffering acts as the fire and hammer that forge our resilience. It tempers us, shapes us, and prepares us for the challenges that lie ahead. The process may be painful, but it is through this refining that we become stronger, wiser, and more capable of enduring life's storms.

For those facing personal struggles, the teachings of Seneca and Marcus Aurelius offer both guidance and solace. They remind us that suffering, while difficult, is not meaningless. It is an opportunity to develop the virtues that define a strong and resilient spirit—courage, patience, humility, and perseverance. By shifting our perspective and seeing adversity as a tool for growth, we reclaim power over our circumstances. We begin to understand that suffering does not diminish us; it transforms us.

This philosophy can be applied in everyday life, whether we are dealing with loss, illness, failure, or uncertainty. Rather than asking, "Why me?" we can ask, "What can I learn from this?" When faced with a setback, we can reframe it as an opportunity to grow stronger or develop a new skill. If we encounter loss, we can choose to honor what remains and find gratitude in what was. By approaching suffering with acceptance and intention, we can turn even life's most difficult moments into opportunities for meaning.

In the words of Marcus Aurelius, "You are not harmed by what happens to you. You are harmed by your opinion of it." This truth lies at the heart of Stoic resilience: suffering is not the enemy. It is a teacher, offering lessons that can guide us toward growth and wisdom. It is in facing hardship that we discover the depth of our strength and the resilience of the human spirit.

The philosophy of suffering and growth is ultimately a call to courage. It challenges us to step into the fire of adversity and trust that, like iron, we will emerge stronger for it. Seneca and Marcus Aurelius understood that suffering is not something to fear but something to embrace as part of life's unfolding journey. Their wisdom invites us to see hardship not as a punishment but as a path—one that leads us to resilience, growth, and the quiet strength that defines the human spirit.

Lessons from Great Lives

Resilience is the quiet strength that carries us

through life's most unrelenting storms. It is the determination to persevere when all seems lost, the hope to rise when circumstances weigh heavily, and the unwavering faith that tomorrow holds possibility. Few people embody this quality more profoundly than Nelson Mandela and Helen Keller—two figures whose lives are testaments to the power of the human spirit. Through unimaginable adversity, they demonstrated that hope and perseverance are not only sources of personal strength but also forces capable of transforming the world.

Nelson Mandela: The Triumph of Hope Over Injustice

Nelson Mandela's life was shaped by hardship and struggle, yet he emerged from decades of injustice as a symbol of forgiveness, perseverance, and reconciliation. Born in South Africa under the oppressive shadow of apartheid, Mandela's early activism placed him on a collision course with a brutal regime determined to suppress his fight for equality. Arrested in 1962 and sentenced to life imprisonment on Robben Island, Mandela spent 27 years in prison. Stripped of his freedom, cut off from his family, and forced into hard labor, his circumstances could have easily broken him. Yet, instead of succumbing to bitterness, Mandela chose to cultivate hope.

Mandela's resilience lay in his ability to reframe his suffering. Imprisonment, while physically confining, became an opportunity to strengthen his mind and spirit. He read widely, reflecting on the works of philosophers, political leaders, and poets. He turned his prison cell into a classroom, mentoring fellow inmates and envisioning a free South Africa where equality would triumph over hatred. Rather than allowing the walls of his cell to confine his purpose, Mandela used them as a crucible to refine his vision.

One of Mandela's most profound lessons was his philosophy of forgiveness. Upon his release in 1990, after nearly three decades behind bars, he stood before the world not as a man consumed by vengeance but as a leader committed to reconciliation. "As I walked out the door toward the gate that would lead to my freedom," Mandela reflected, "I knew if I didn't leave my bitterness and hatred behind, I'd still be in prison." These words reveal a universal truth: resentment can imprison the spirit as effectively as any physical walls. By choosing forgiveness, Mandela liberated himself and his nation, proving that resilience is not just about survival but about rising with grace and purpose.

For readers confronting their own struggles— whether personal loss, injustice, or setbacks— Mandela's life offers a guiding light. Resilience is not the absence of pain but the ability to respond with hope. When circumstances feel overwhelming, Mandela teaches us to focus on what we can control: our mindset, our actions, and our ability to rise above bitterness. His life reminds us that perseverance is not only an act of endurance but also an act of transformation. By choosing hope, even when it seems impossible, we reclaim our power and create the possibility for change.

Helen Keller: Finding Light in the Darkest of Circumstances

Helen Keller's story is one of extraordinary triumph over seemingly insurmountable odds. Born in 1880, Keller lost her sight and hearing at just 19 months old due to illness. Locked in a world of silence and darkness, she faced isolation so profound that many believed she could never learn, communicate, or engage meaningfully with the world. Yet, through sheer determination and the unwavering support of her teacher, Anne Sullivan, Keller overcame her limitations and became a global symbol of resilience, courage, and hope.

Keller's breakthrough came when Sullivan introduced her to the concept of language, spelling the word "water" into her hand while running water over it. This moment unlocked a pathway for Keller to connect with the world around her. She would later describe this experience as a rebirth—an awakening to the infinite possibilities of the mind and spirit. Keller went on to become the first deaf-blind person to earn a college degree, a prolific writer, and an advocate for people with disabilities, traveling the world to inspire millions with her story.

What makes Keller's life so remarkable is not just her triumph over physical adversity but her perspective on hardship. "Although the world is full of suffering," she once wrote, "it is full also of the overcoming of it." For Keller, suffering was not an endpoint but a beginning—a catalyst for growth, learning, and discovery. She refused to be defined by her limitations, instead choosing to focus on what she could achieve. Her life serves as a powerful reminder that resilience is not about the absence of struggle but about the refusal to surrender to it.

Keller's philosophy also highlights the importance of purpose in overcoming adversity. She dedicated her life to serving others, advocating for equal rights, education, and opportunities for people with disabilities. In finding meaning beyond herself, Keller transformed her suffering into a gift for the world. Her story reminds us that purpose can arise from even the darkest circumstances, and it is often in serving others that we find the strength to persevere.

For those facing personal challenges, Keller's life offers a profound lesson: limitations—whether physical, emotional, or circumstantial—are not barriers to purpose but opportunities for growth. When we choose to focus on possibility rather than limitation, we discover untapped reservoirs of strength within ourselves. Keller's story encourages us to see adversity not as an obstacle but as a chance to overcome, to inspire, and to rise beyond what we believed possible.

Resilience as a Choice

Both Nelson Mandela and Helen Keller exemplify the profound resilience of the human spirit. Their lives show us that while adversity is inevitable, our response to it is a choice. Mandela chose hope over hatred, forgiveness over resentment. Keller chose discovery over despair, service over isolation. Their examples challenge us to reflect on our own struggles: How can I reframe this hardship as an opportunity for growth? How can I use my challenges to inspire others and contribute to the world?

The stories of these great lives also highlight a central truth about resilience: it is not a solitary journey. Mandela leaned on the community of his fellow inmates and the dream of a united South Africa. Keller found strength in her teacher, Anne Sullivan, and the people who believed in her potential. Resilience is forged not in isolation but in connection—with others, with our purpose, and with the belief that even in the face of adversity, we have the power to create meaning.

In their lives, we see that resilience is not about avoiding suffering but about responding to it with courage, hope, and perseverance. Mandela and Keller teach us that no challenge is insurmountable, no obstacle too great to overcome. Their stories remind us that the human spirit, when fortified with purpose and hope, can rise above even the darkest of circumstances.

For readers confronting their own trials, the lives of these extraordinary individuals offer both inspiration and guidance. Their resilience challenges us to find light in darkness, strength in struggle, and purpose in pain. In doing so, we honor the enduring truth they both embodied: that within each of us lies the power to overcome, to grow, and to rise—no matter the odds.

The Role of Mindset in Adversity

In the face of adversity, our mindset can be the difference between crumbling under the weight of our challenges and emerging stronger because of them. While we cannot always control the circumstances that life presents us, we can control how we respond to them. This principle lies at the heart of both Stoic philosophy and modern psychology, which teach us that the key to resilience often rests in how we think. By shifting our mindset, we can transform obstacles into opportunities, setbacks into lessons, and suffering into growth.

The ancient Stoic philosopher Epictetus was born into slavery and lived much of his early life in chains. Yet, despite his external hardships, Epictetus discovered a profound truth: our thoughts and judgments, not our circumstances, determine our experience of life. "We are disturbed not by events, but by the views we take of them," he taught. To Epictetus, suffering was not rooted in the adversity itself but in how we perceived it. The moment we recognize that our minds are within our control, we reclaim power over our lives, no matter the situation.

For example, if we experience failure, we might be tempted to see it as a sign of inadequacy—a source of shame or regret. This interpretation fuels despair and inaction, trapping us in negativity. But by shifting our mindset, as Epictetus suggests, we can view failure differently: as a necessary step toward growth, as feedback for improvement, or as evidence that we dared to try. The event remains the same, but our response transforms its impact. In this way, mindset becomes a tool for resilience, helping us endure hardship with clarity, wisdom, and grace.

Modern psychology has given this ancient insight a scientific foundation. Cognitive Behavioral Therapy (CBT), developed by psychologist Aaron Beck, is built on the understanding that our thoughts shape our emotions and behaviors. CBT teaches individuals to challenge and reframe negative thought patterns, replacing them with healthier, more constructive perspectives. For instance, a person facing a job loss might initially think, "I'll never recover from this," which leads to feelings of hopelessness and stagnation. By shifting this thought to, "This is difficult, but it's also an opportunity to explore a new path," they begin to reclaim agency and open themselves to growth.

Psychologist Carol Dweck's research on the "growth mindset" further underscores the transformative power of perspective. Dweck found that individuals who view challenges as opportunities to learn and develop are more likely to persevere through adversity. In contrast, those with a "fixed mindset" — who see abilities and circumstances as unchangeable — tend to avoid challenges for fear of failure. The growth mindset fosters resilience by encouraging us to see effort as valuable, mistakes as lessons, and struggles as pathways to improvement. "The view you adopt for yourself profoundly affects the way you lead your life," Dweck writes. Her work reinforces what Epictetus taught centuries ago: by changing our perspective, we change our experience.

Consider the story of Thomas Edison, whose relentless optimism exemplifies the power of a growth mindset. Edison, when working to perfect the lightbulb, reportedly conducted over a thousand unsuccessful experiments before finding success. Yet, when asked about his repeated failures, he famously replied, "I have not failed. I've just found 10,000 ways that won't work." Edison's mindset transformed failure into progress, allowing him to persevere where others might have given up. His example illustrates a powerful truth: adversity is not the end of the road; it is a detour on the path to achievement.

Epictetus would recognize this spirit in Edison's approach. To him, the external "failure" was irrelevant—what mattered was the mindset that shaped the response. By focusing on what was within his control (his effort, his determination, and his perspective), Edison turned his challenges into opportunities for discovery and growth.

The role of mindset in overcoming adversity is especially critical in moments when life feels overwhelming or unfair. Viktor Frankl, whose wisdom has already been explored in earlier sections, captured this beautifully when he wrote, "When we are no longer able to change a situation, we are challenged to change ourselves." Frankl's experience in Nazi concentration camps revealed that while external suffering may be unavoidable, our inner response—our mindset—remains within our control. He observed that those who found a sense of purpose and maintained hope often endured far more than seemed possible. Frankl's words remind us that resilience is not about denying pain but about reframing it as an opportunity to demonstrate strength and meaning.

The practice of shifting our mindset can be applied to everyday struggles as well. When facing a difficult relationship, a health crisis, or career setbacks, the challenge is to pause and ask: *What can I learn from this? How can this experience help me grow?* This act of reframing does not diminish the pain of adversity, but it changes its power over us. Rather than being victims of our circumstances, we become active participants in shaping our responses and finding meaning in the struggle.

The Japanese philosophy of *shikata ga nai*, which translates to "it cannot be helped," echoes this principle of acceptance and reframing. *Shikata ga nai* teaches that while some events are beyond our control—loss, illness, failure—we still have the choice to respond with dignity and resolve. Instead of resisting what cannot be changed, we adapt to it, finding peace and purpose in the midst of challenge. This mindset aligns perfectly with Stoic teachings and modern psychology, both of which emphasize the importance of acceptance and action.

For those looking to cultivate a resilient mindset,

practical steps can begin with small, intentional shifts in perspective. When adversity strikes, pause to reflect: *Is my interpretation of this event helping or hurting me? What can I control in this moment? How can I view this challenge as an opportunity?* By asking these questions, we reframe our experience, reclaim our agency, and open ourselves to growth.

Epictetus and modern psychologists agree that adversity itself is not the enemy—our mindset determines whether it defeats us or empowers us. With practice, the mind becomes a tool for resilience, allowing us to transform even life's most difficult challenges into opportunities for strength, learning, and meaning.

In the end, the role of mindset in adversity is both profound and empowering. By changing how we think, we change how we experience hardship. Challenges become teachers. Failures become steps toward success. Suffering becomes a path to wisdom. As Epictetus reminds us, "The greater the difficulty, the more glory in surmounting it." Through the lens of a resilient mindset, adversity is not a curse but a gift—an opportunity to rise, to grow, and to uncover the depths of our strength.

Overcoming Personal Obstacles

Life's obstacles come in countless forms—grief, failure, illness, or uncertainty—but their impact is universal. When we encounter challenges, it can feel as though we are standing before an immovable wall, with no clear path forward. Yet history's greatest thinkers, alongside modern insights, reveal that obstacles are not endpoints. They are opportunities—tests of character that, when approached with intention and wisdom, can shape us into stronger, more resilient versions of ourselves. From the Stoic practices of self-discipline and perspective to modern strategies grounded in psychology, overcoming personal struggles begins with one powerful realization: the human spirit is capable of far more than we often believe.

The Stoic philosopher Epictetus, who began life as a slave in ancient Rome, offers some of the most timeless and practical advice for navigating personal hardships. His core teaching centers on the distinction between what is within our control and what is not. "Some things are up to us, and some are not up to us," he observed. Our thoughts, actions, and choices remain fully within our power, while external events—misfortune, loss, or the actions of others—lie beyond it. Epictetus taught that freedom is found not in controlling the world but in mastering our responses to it.

Imagine, for instance, someone who has just lost a job—a deeply personal and often disorienting obstacle. It is easy to spiral into frustration, blame, or despair, all of which focus on the uncontrollable aspects of the situation. Yet Epictetus would remind us to shift our attention inward. What remains within our power? Our effort to search for new opportunities. Our mindset and outlook as we navigate the transition. Our ability to learn from the experience and adapt. By focusing on what we can control, we reclaim agency, even when life feels beyond our grasp. Obstacles lose their power when we recognize that our response to them is ours to shape.

Modern psychology reinforces this philosophy through the concept of *response flexibility*—the capacity to pause and choose how we react to a challenge. Viktor Frankl, whose wisdom often bridges ancient philosophy and modern psychology, wrote that "between stimulus and response, there is a space. In that space is our power to choose our response. In our response lies our growth and our freedom." By creating this mental space—whether through mindfulness, reflection, or deliberate choice—we can transform impulsive reactions into intentional actions, ensuring that obstacles become opportunities for growth rather than sources of defeat.

One practical approach to cultivating this power is reframing—a strategy drawn from cognitive behavioral therapy (CBT). Reframing challenges us to shift how we perceive a difficult situation, much like turning a prism to see light from a new angle. Consider the story of Thomas Edison, who famously described his countless failed attempts to invent the lightbulb as "10,000 steps to success." Rather than viewing failure as evidence of inadequacy, Edison chose to see it as a necessary part of progress. This shift in perspective is available to all of us. Obstacles may remain, but our perception of them determines whether they become barriers or stepping stones.

Modern-day thinkers like Carol Dweck have further explored this transformative power of perception through the concept of the "growth mindset." Dweck's research reveals that individuals who believe abilities and circumstances can change through effort are far more resilient in the face of setbacks. A fixed mindset—one that views challenges as threats or unchangeable—traps us in stagnation. But a growth mindset reframes adversity as an opportunity to learn, adapt, and strengthen. The obstacle becomes a chance to grow into a better version of ourselves, rather than a sign of defeat.

For example, a student struggling with a difficult subject may initially see their challenges as evidence of failure. With a growth mindset, however, they shift their focus: "This is hard because I'm learning something new. With effort and practice, I will improve." By embracing effort and persistence, they transform the obstacle into a gateway for progress. This mindset, while simple in theory, requires intentional practice. It asks us to look at our struggles—no matter how uncomfortable—and ask, *What can this teach me? How can I grow through this?*

Philosopher Friedrich Nietzsche captured this lesson in his often-quoted phrase, "What does not kill me makes me stronger." While the sentiment may sound blunt, Nietzsche's deeper point is profound: adversity, when faced with resilience and courage, builds inner fortitude. It teaches us patience, adaptability, and the ability to endure life's uncertainties. The struggles we overcome become the foundation upon which we stand—proof that we are capable of enduring and thriving, even in the face of difficulty.

This idea resonates deeply in the lives of individuals who have turned personal struggles into sources of strength. Consider J.K. Rowling, who wrote *Harry Potter* while navigating the depths of poverty, rejection, and personal loss. Reflecting on her journey, she noted, "Rock bottom became the solid foundation on which I rebuilt my life." Her story underscores a powerful truth: when we face adversity head-on, we often uncover untapped strength and creativity within ourselves. Struggles, far from diminishing us, can reveal the best of what we are capable of achieving.

For readers confronting their own obstacles, practical strategies can help transform adversity into growth. The first step is acceptance—acknowledging the reality of the challenge without resistance. Marcus Aurelius reminds us, "The universe is change; our life is what our thoughts make it." By accepting what is, we free ourselves to focus on what can be done. Next, reflection becomes a tool for transformation. Ask yourself: *What can I learn from this? How can this struggle make me stronger?* Writing down answers can provide clarity, helping to reframe the obstacle as an opportunity for growth.

Finally, small, intentional actions—no matter how modest—can shift momentum. Resilience is built step by step, through choices that move us forward. Whether it's taking a single action toward a goal, reaching out for support, or simply choosing to get up and try again, these small acts of courage remind us that we are not powerless in the face of hardship.

Ultimately, overcoming personal obstacles is a process of transformation. It is not about eliminating struggles but about meeting them with courage, intention, and the belief that growth is possible. The wisdom of Epictetus, modern psychology, and countless stories of resilience remind us that hardship, while inevitable, is not insurmountable. Through acceptance, reframing, and action, we learn to navigate life's obstacles with grace.

In doing so, we discover a deeper truth: the challenges we face are not barriers to our growth—they are the very path to it. It is through adversity that we cultivate resilience, strengthen our character, and uncover the boundless potential of the human spirit. As Epictetus so eloquently reminds us, "The greater the difficulty, the more glory in surmounting it." With the right mindset, every obstacle becomes an opportunity to rise, to grow, and to become the person we were meant to be.

CHAPTER 5: LIVING AUTHENTICALLY – THE COURAGE TO BE YOURSELF

Philosophical Foundations of Authenticity

To live authentically is to live in harmony with one's truest self—a life shaped not by societal expectations but by inner truth. Yet, this ideal is as challenging as it is timeless. Across the ages, philosophers have wrestled with the tension between individuality and conformity, offering wisdom that remains profoundly relevant today. Socrates, Ralph Waldo Emerson, and Friedrich Nietzsche, though separated by centuries and cultures, converge on a singular truth: embracing one's individuality requires courage, introspection, and an unwavering commitment to truth. Authenticity, they teach us, is not simply about self-expression—it is about living in alignment with who we are, no matter the cost.

Socrates, often regarded as the father of Western philosophy, laid the foundation for understanding authenticity through his relentless pursuit of self-knowledge. In ancient Athens, a society that prized reputation, tradition, and status, Socrates challenged individuals to turn their gaze inward. "Know thyself," he urged—a simple yet radical call to examine one's beliefs, values, and actions with unflinching honesty. For Socrates, living authentically meant aligning one's life with reason and virtue rather than blindly following societal norms.

His commitment to this principle was so unwavering that it cost him his life. When accused of corrupting the youth of Athens and disrespecting the gods, Socrates was given the chance to renounce his teachings in exchange for his freedom. Yet he refused, declaring that to abandon his pursuit of truth would betray his very self. "I cannot and will not cut my conscience to fit this year's fashions," he said. For Socrates, the courage to live authentically — to uphold his principles even in the face of death — was the highest expression of a life well lived. His example reminds us that authenticity is not always easy or convenient. It demands that we prioritize integrity over acceptance and truth over comfort.

Centuries later, Ralph Waldo Emerson, the American transcendentalist, expanded on Socratic ideas, offering a vision of authenticity rooted in self-reliance and individuality. In his seminal essay *Self-Reliance*, Emerson declared,

"To be yourself in a world that is constantly trying to make you something else is the greatest accomplishment." For Emerson, authenticity was the antidote to conformity—the tendency to suppress our true selves in order to fit into society's mold. He believed that each person possessed a unique "divine spark"—an inner voice that, if followed, would lead to a life of purpose and fulfillment.

Emerson's philosophy was deeply personal. He rejected the notion that external validation or approval could determine one's worth, arguing instead that true strength came from trusting one's instincts and convictions. "Trust thyself: every heart vibrates to that iron string," he wrote, urging readers to listen to their inner wisdom rather than seeking guidance from the crowd. Emerson understood that the pursuit of authenticity often meant standing alone, risking criticism, and resisting the pressure to conform. Yet he believed that this risk was worth the reward: a life that is fully one's own.

In today's world, where social media amplifies the pressure to conform and curate an image that pleases others, Emerson's call for self-reliance feels particularly urgent. His teachings challenge us to look beyond superficial measures of success and embrace the courage to live according to our values, passions, and truths. By trusting ourselves, we reclaim the power to shape our lives authentically, regardless of external expectations.

Friedrich Nietzsche, the German philosopher whose work often startled and unsettled his contemporaries, offered a more provocative exploration of authenticity. For Nietzsche, living authentically meant transcending societal norms and embracing the full expression of one's individuality. He introduced the concept of the *Übermensch*—the "overman" or "superman"— as an ideal of human potential. The *Übermensch*, according to Nietzsche, was an individual who rejected imposed values and created their own meaning, unshackled by tradition or conformity.

Nietzsche's philosophy emerged in response to what he saw as the decay of individuality in modern society. He criticized the "herd mentality"—a phenomenon in which people sacrifice their individuality to follow the crowd, choosing comfort and mediocrity over risk and greatness. To Nietzsche, the pursuit of authenticity required rebellion against this collective inertia. "Become who you are," he famously declared, urging individuals to confront their fears, embrace their complexity, and live with unapologetic intensity.

This idea resonates powerfully for those who feel trapped by expectations, whether imposed by family, culture, or their own self-doubt. Nietzsche's vision of authenticity calls us to break free from these constraints and become the architects of our lives. He invites us to ask: Are we living according to our own values, or are we merely following the script written for us by others? Are we expressing our truest selves, or are we hiding behind a mask of acceptability? By confronting these questions, we take the first step toward authentic living.

While Nietzsche's philosophy may seem demanding, it offers a liberating truth: authenticity is not about perfection but about the willingness to embrace one's full humanity—the strengths, the flaws, the contradictions. It is about having the courage to be seen as we are, not as we think we should be.

Taken together, the teachings of Socrates, Emerson, and Nietzsche reveal a powerful path to authenticity. Socrates teaches us the importance of self-examination and integrity—of knowing ourselves and living in accordance with that knowledge. Emerson inspires us to trust our instincts and reject conformity, reminding us that our uniqueness is our strength. Nietzsche challenges us to create our own meaning and embrace life with boldness, even when it demands discomfort.

In practical terms, living authentically begins with small, intentional choices. It means asking ourselves: *What do I truly value? What brings me joy and meaning?* It requires the courage to say no to what does not align with our values and yes to what does, even when it feels uncertain or difficult. It invites us to embrace our individuality, to honor our passions, and to express our truths, knowing that the reward is a life of fulfillment and purpose.

For those who feel the weight of external expectations, these philosophical foundations serve as a reminder: authenticity is not something to be granted by others; it is something to be claimed by ourselves. As Socrates, Emerson, and Nietzsche demonstrate, the journey to authenticity may be challenging, but it is also one of the most courageous and rewarding pursuits we can undertake. In embracing who we truly are, we unlock the freedom to live a life that is fully, unapologetically our own.

Rejecting Conformity and External Expectations

To live authentically, one must first confront the powerful forces of conformity—those subtle and overt pressures that encourage us to trade individuality for acceptance, security, or approval. From societal norms to cultural expectations, external forces often seek to shape our lives in ways that align with collective standards rather than personal truth. Yet history's great thinkers, from Henry David Thoreau to existentialist philosophers like Jean-Paul Sartre and Simone de Beauvoir, remind us that breaking free from these pressures is not only a choice but a moral imperative. Living authentically requires us to step outside the comfortable confines of conformity, even when it means risking disapproval, uncertainty, or solitude.

Henry David Thoreau's life and work exemplify the courage it takes to reject external expectations and live in harmony with one's inner values. In 1845, Thoreau withdrew from society to live in a small cabin on the shores of Walden Pond. His two-year experiment in simplicity and self-reliance became the basis for his seminal work, *Walden*. Thoreau's decision was not an escape but a deliberate act of resistance—a rejection of the materialism, noise, and superficiality of his time. "I went to the woods because I wished to live deliberately, to front only the essential facts of life," he wrote. "I wanted to live deep and suck out all the marrow of life."

Thoreau's retreat was not about isolation but about clarity. He sought to strip life down to its essentials, free from the distractions and demands of a society that prioritized wealth, status, and conformity over meaning and purpose. By choosing a life aligned with his values, he demonstrated that authenticity requires both introspection and action. Thoreau's experiment challenges us to ask: *What do I truly need? What distractions or expectations prevent me from living authentically?*

Yet rejecting conformity often demands more than solitude—it requires the willingness to face discomfort. Thoreau himself was no stranger to conflict. He refused to pay poll taxes that funded slavery and the Mexican-American War, leading to his arrest. "Under a government which imprisons any unjustly, the true place for a just man is also a prison," he wrote in *Civil Disobedience*. His resistance highlights an essential truth: to live authentically, we must sometimes stand alone. By refusing to align with values that conflicted with his own, Thoreau embodied the courage to act according to his conscience, regardless of the consequences.

The existentialist philosophers of the 20th century took Thoreau's principles further, exploring the internal struggle individuals face when seeking authenticity in a world that imposes expectations. Jean-Paul Sartre, the father of existentialism, argued that freedom is both a gift and a burden. To Sartre, individuals are condemned to be free—compelled to take responsibility for their choices, even when doing so creates discomfort or uncertainty. "Man is nothing else but what he makes of himself," he declared, rejecting the notion that we are defined by societal roles, traditions, or circumstances.

For Sartre, conformity represented a denial of freedom—an avoidance of the responsibility to choose one's path. He described this avoidance as *bad faith*, a state in which individuals deceive themselves into believing they have no choice but to live according to external expectations. For example, someone who remains in an unfulfilling career because it is "what society expects" may convince themselves they have no alternative. Sartre challenges us to see this for what it is: a refusal to embrace the radical freedom we possess to shape our lives. Authentic living, he argued, requires us to confront this freedom and take ownership of who we are, even when the path ahead is uncertain.

Simone de Beauvoir, Sartre's contemporary and fellow existentialist, extended this idea to the realm of identity, particularly for women. In *The Second Sex*, de Beauvoir critiqued how societal expectations often reduce women to predefined roles—mother, wife, or caregiver—limiting their ability to express their full humanity. "One is not born, but rather becomes, a woman," she wrote, highlighting how external pressures shape identity. To live authentically, de Beauvoir argued, women must reject these imposed definitions and define themselves on their own terms. Her philosophy speaks to all who feel constrained by societal labels, urging us to break free from roles that diminish our individuality.

The struggle to reject conformity remains as relevant today as it was for Thoreau, Sartre, and de Beauvoir. In a world of curated social media feeds, cultural pressures, and constant comparison, the temptation to conform can be overwhelming. We are encouraged to fit in, to follow prescribed paths, and to measure success according to external standards—status, wealth, or popularity. Yet these pressures often lead to lives that feel hollow, disconnected from who we truly are. Authenticity demands that we question these narratives and choose a life aligned with our deepest values, even when it means diverging from the crowd.

Practically, rejecting conformity begins with small acts of courage. It means asking ourselves hard questions: *Am I making this choice because it is true to me, or because it is expected of me?* It requires us to listen to our intuition, to recognize when we are acting out of fear or a desire for approval, and to have the courage to step off the well-trodden path. Like Thoreau, we might need to retreat—perhaps not to a literal cabin, but to a space of stillness and reflection where we can reconnect with what truly matters.

It also requires action. Sartre and de Beauvoir remind us that authenticity is not a passive state but an ongoing process of choice. To live authentically, we must be willing to risk judgment, rejection, or failure. We must say no to what does not serve us and yes to what does, even when the path is uncertain. In doing so, we reclaim our freedom—the freedom to define ourselves and to live lives that are fully, unapologetically our own.

Consider the artist Vincent van Gogh, whose life exemplifies this struggle. Rejected by critics during his lifetime, van Gogh continued to paint with relentless passion, driven not by external approval but by an inner need to express his truth. "If you hear a voice within you say you cannot paint, then by all means paint," he wrote, "and that voice will be silenced." His commitment to authenticity, despite ridicule and poverty, left behind a legacy that continues to inspire. Van Gogh's story reminds us that authenticity is not about pleasing others but about honoring the voice within us, no matter how faint or unconventional it may seem.

In the end, rejecting conformity is an act of liberation. It frees us from the weight of external expectations and allows us to live with integrity, passion, and purpose. The teachings of Thoreau, Sartre, and de Beauvoir challenge us to break free from the roles, labels, and pressures that confine us. They remind us that the path to authenticity is not always easy, but it is always worth it. For when we choose to live true to ourselves, we discover a life of meaning, freedom, and profound fulfillment.

The Power of Vulnerability

To live authentically requires not only the courage to be oneself but also the willingness to embrace vulnerability—the parts of us we often hide in an attempt to appear strong, perfect, or unshakable. Vulnerability, however, is not a weakness; it is a profound source of strength, connection, and freedom. In a world that rewards invulnerability—polished appearances, flawless performances, and emotional armor—choosing to show up with our imperfections requires extraordinary bravery. Thinkers like Brené Brown, alongside historical leaders who demonstrated vulnerability in action, remind us that to be vulnerable is to be truly alive, unshackled from the fear of judgment or failure.

Brené Brown, the modern-day researcher and storyteller whose work has reframed our understanding of vulnerability, describes it as "uncertainty, risk, and emotional exposure." In her groundbreaking book *Daring Greatly*, Brown argues that vulnerability is the birthplace of authenticity, creativity, and meaningful relationships. "Vulnerability is not winning or losing," she writes. "It's having the courage to show up and be seen when we have no control over the outcome." For Brown, vulnerability is at the core of living authentically because it asks us to remove the masks we wear to protect ourselves and share who we really are—flaws, fears, and all.

Brown's work is deeply influenced by Theodore Roosevelt's famous "Man in the Arena" speech, which celebrates the individual who dares greatly despite the risk of failure. "The credit belongs to the man who is actually in the arena," Roosevelt proclaimed, "who errs, who comes short again and again, because there is no effort without error and shortcoming." Roosevelt's words capture the essence of vulnerability: to step into the arena of life—to take risks, expose ourselves to uncertainty, and face potential criticism—is to embrace the fullness of our humanity. Brown reframes this as an invitation to live wholeheartedly, to recognize that perfection is an illusion and that our imperfections are what make us real, relatable, and resilient.

Historical leaders exemplify how embracing vulnerability can create powerful connections and inspire lasting change. Consider Abraham Lincoln, who led the United States through its darkest hours during the Civil War. Lincoln's authenticity lay in his willingness to share his doubts, fears, and struggles openly, even while carrying the weight of a fractured nation. In his private letters, Lincoln expressed deep anguish over the loss of life and the seemingly endless conflict, revealing a man who felt the full weight of his responsibility. Yet far from diminishing his strength, Lincoln's vulnerability humanized him. It allowed him to connect with a divided people not as a distant figure of authority but as a leader who shared in their pain and uncertainty.

This capacity for vulnerability was also a hallmark of Mahatma Gandhi, whose philosophy of nonviolence, or *ahimsa*, relied on the strength of authenticity and emotional exposure. Gandhi's refusal to retaliate in the face of oppression required immense courage, as he allowed himself—and his followers—to be seen in moments of great vulnerability. By choosing nonviolence, Gandhi revealed the raw humanity of those oppressed and challenged the moral conscience of the oppressors. His vulnerability became a powerful tool for transformation, demonstrating that strength is not found in domination but in the courage to remain true to one's values, even in the face of suffering.

These leaders show us that vulnerability does not diminish our strength—it amplifies it. When we allow ourselves to be seen, imperfections and all, we inspire trust, connection, and courage in others. Vulnerability breaks down the barriers of pretense and invites authenticity into our relationships, our work, and our lives.

In our modern world, where perfectionism and curated appearances dominate, the pressure to conceal our vulnerabilities can feel overwhelming. Social media, workplace competition, and cultural expectations encourage us to project strength while hiding our struggles. Yet Brené Brown's research reveals a paradox: the very qualities we hide—our fears, mistakes, and uncertainties—are often the keys to building deeper relationships and living more fulfilling lives. When we allow ourselves to say, "I don't know," "I need help," or "I made a mistake," we open the door to connection, growth, and healing.

This truth is illustrated in the realm of art and creativity, where vulnerability is essential. Take the work of Frida Kahlo, whose deeply personal paintings exposed her physical and emotional pain. Kahlo's art, raw and unapologetically honest, resonated with millions because it revealed her humanity. By embracing her vulnerabilities—her struggles with identity, illness, and heartbreak—she created a legacy that transcends her suffering. Her willingness to "be seen" reminds us that vulnerability is a bridge: it connects our innermost experiences with those of others, creating shared understanding and compassion.

Practical wisdom for embracing vulnerability begins with self-acceptance. It requires us to let go of perfectionism and the need for approval, recognizing that our imperfections do not make us less worthy but more human. Instead of asking, "What will others think?" we can ask, "What is true for me in this moment?" This shift allows us to prioritize authenticity over appearances, creating space for deeper connection with ourselves and those around us.

For example, someone struggling to admit failure might fear being seen as weak or incompetent. Yet by acknowledging the failure honestly—"I made a mistake, and I'm learning from it"—they model humility and courage. This act of vulnerability often inspires others to do the same, creating an environment of trust and growth. Whether in personal relationships, creative pursuits, or professional settings, vulnerability invites others to show up fully as themselves, fostering stronger bonds and deeper understanding.

Living authentically requires us to embrace vulnerability as an essential part of the journey. It means having the courage to share our stories, even when they feel imperfect. It means showing up to life's challenges without certainty but with intention and heart. As Brené Brown reminds us, "What makes you vulnerable makes you beautiful." Our willingness to be seen, to risk, and to embrace imperfection is what makes us real, courageous, and ultimately, free.

In embracing vulnerability, we reclaim our humanity. We learn that true strength lies not in hiding our flaws but in owning them. We discover that authenticity is not about being perfect but about being whole—flawed, resilient, and beautifully imperfect. The power of vulnerability lies in its ability to transform: to turn fear into courage, isolation into connection, and imperfection into a source of meaning and beauty. It is through this embrace of vulnerability that we find the courage to live authentically, to step

into the arena, and to show up fully for the lives
we are meant to live.

Authenticity in Action

Living authentically is not merely a philosophy
but a way of being—an ongoing, courageous
act that shapes not only our lives but also the
world around us. History is filled with individuals who dared to embody their truest selves,
even when doing so demanded immense courage. Through their authenticity, these artists,
innovators, and revolutionaries broke boundaries, inspired change, and proved that living
courageously yields rewards far greater than
conformity ever could. Their stories illuminate
the power of authenticity in action, offering us
both guidance and inspiration.

Take Vincent van Gogh, whose unwavering
commitment to his artistic vision exemplifies
the struggle—and ultimate reward—of living
authentically. Born into modest circumstances
and rejected repeatedly by critics during his
lifetime, van Gogh refused to compromise his
style to suit public taste. His bold, expressive
brushstrokes and vivid colors were unlike any-

thing seen in his time, leading many to dismiss his work as unrefined or even "mad." Yet van Gogh remained resolute. His letters reveal a man deeply committed to his truth: "What would life be if we had no courage to attempt anything?"

Despite living in poverty, battling mental illness, and facing relentless rejection, van Gogh found purpose in his authenticity. He painted not for acclaim but because it was an inseparable part of who he was. "I put my heart and soul into my work," he wrote, "and have lost my mind in the process." Today, van Gogh is celebrated as one of history's greatest artists, his work a testament to the enduring power of authenticity. His story reminds us that living courageously may come at a cost, but the rewards—integrity, meaning, and the possibility of leaving a lasting legacy—are priceless.

Authenticity also lies at the heart of innovation. Consider the story of Steve Jobs, the visionary behind Apple. Jobs' refusal to conform to conventional business practices and his insistence on blending technology with artistry revolutionized the world. He was not afraid to challenge norms, reject mediocrity, and demand excellence, even when others doubted his vision. "Your time is limited," Jobs famously said, "so don't waste it living someone else's life. Have the courage to follow your heart and intuition." Jobs' authenticity—his refusal to settle for anything less than his ideals—transformed not only his life but also the lives of millions. His story teaches us that innovation begins with the courage to think differently, to trust one's instincts, and to remain true to a personal vision, no matter the opposition.

Revolutionaries, too, are defined by their authenticity. Rosa Parks, often called the "mother of the civil rights movement," demonstrated extraordinary courage by refusing to surrender her bus seat to a white passenger in 1955. Her act was deceptively simple yet profoundly authentic: Parks chose to honor her dignity and stand by her principles in a society that demanded silence and submission. "I had no idea that history was being made," she reflected later. "I was just tired of giving in." Parks' refusal to conform ignited a movement that transformed the fabric of society, proving that authenticity in action—even in a single, quiet moment—can inspire monumental change.

Her story offers an enduring lesson: living authentically often requires standing up for what is right, even when the world stands against you. Parks' courage was not born from grand ambition but from an unshakable sense of self and a refusal to betray her truth. She reminds us that authenticity is not always loud or dramatic—it is the quiet resolve to align one's actions with one's values, no matter the circumstances.

Artists, innovators, and revolutionaries may occupy different spheres, but they share a common thread: the willingness to risk rejection, failure, or hardship to remain true to themselves. Their stories challenge us to reflect on our own lives: *What parts of myself am I hiding to please others? What truths am I afraid to express? What dreams have I abandoned out of fear?* Living authentically requires us to confront these questions with honesty and resolve.

Yet authenticity is not reserved for the famous or extraordinary. Its power is available to all of us, in the smallest acts of courage. It is found in the musician who creates work that reflects their heart, even if no one listens. It exists in the

entrepreneur who starts a business based on
their passion, despite the risks. It appears in the
parent who teaches their children to embrace
their uniqueness, or the student who chooses
an unconventional path because it aligns with
their truth. Authenticity does not require fame,
wealth, or recognition—it requires the willingness to be seen as we truly are.

Practical wisdom for putting authenticity into
action begins with embracing discomfort. Living authentically often feels risky because it requires us to step outside the safety of conformity
and face the possibility of judgment or failure.
Yet discomfort is a sign of growth—a signal that
we are moving closer to who we truly are. The
poet E.E. Cummings captured this beautifully
when he wrote, "It takes courage to grow up
and become who you really are."

It also requires patience. Authenticity is not a
destination but a process—a series of choices,
big and small, that reflect our deepest values.
We may not always get it right, and we will face
moments of doubt. Yet each time we choose
authenticity, we strengthen our ability to live
courageously. We reclaim our freedom to shape

our lives according to what matters most.

The rewards of living authentically extend far beyond personal fulfillment. When we embrace our truth, we inspire others to do the same. Rosa Parks' quiet refusal sparked a movement. Steve Jobs' commitment to his vision redefined technology. Van Gogh's unapologetic expression continues to move hearts. Their stories remind us that authenticity has a ripple effect: it creates space for others to show up fully, to challenge norms, and to live with purpose.

In the end, authenticity in action is about showing up as we are, embracing our uniqueness, and trusting that our truth has value. It is about recognizing that the world does not need more people who conform—it needs people who are willing to live courageously, to dare greatly, and to leave a mark that is uniquely their own. As Steve Jobs so powerfully reminded us, "The people who are crazy enough to think they can change the world are the ones who do."

When we choose to live authentically, we join those who dared to stand apart, to challenge expectations, and to create something meaningful.

We step into our own arena, imperfections and all, and discover the freedom, connection, and fulfillment that come from living a life true to ourselves. It is through this courage—this refusal to hide or compromise—that we honor not only our own potential but also the possibilities we create for those around us.

CHAPTER 6:
THE POWER OF
CONNECTION
– LESSONS ON
BUILDING COMMUNITY
AND BELONGING

The Importance of Human Connection

At the core of the human experience lies a profound truth: we are not meant to navigate life alone. From ancient philosophy to modern psychology, thinkers across time and cultures have emphasized the centrality of human connection in achieving fulfillment, meaning, and well-being. Whether in Aristotle's view of humans as inherently "social animals," Confucian teachings on harmony, or contemporary research on belonging, the message is clear: connection is not just desirable—it is essential. It is through relationships and community that we discover who we are, strengthen our resilience, and shape the world around us.

Aristotle, one of history's most influential philosophers, identified human connection as fundamental to our nature. In his *Politics*, he declared that "man is by nature a social animal," emphasizing that humans are intrinsically inclined toward relationships and community. To Aristotle, the individual cannot exist in isolation; we are designed to live together, to collaborate, and to thrive within a shared social framework.

He believed that the highest form of human life is realized not in solitude but in relationships that foster virtue, mutual support, and purpose.

Aristotle also explored the concept of *eudaimonia*, often translated as "human flourishing." He argued that flourishing is achieved through meaningful engagement with others—through friendships, family, and participation in the larger community. For Aristotle, a good life is not defined by wealth or power but by the quality of one's relationships. Genuine connection, rooted in shared values and mutual respect, enables individuals to grow and become their best selves. This wisdom challenges us to ask: *Am I nurturing relationships that contribute to my flourishing and that of others?*

In Eastern philosophy, Confucius offered a complementary perspective on connection, emphasizing harmony, reciprocity, and collective well-being. For Confucius, relationships were not simply a matter of individual fulfillment but the foundation of a harmonious society. His teachings, compiled in the *Analects*, stressed the importance of honoring roles within families, friendships, and communities to create balance and mutual respect. Confucius believed that when individuals prioritize connection and harmony, society as a whole flourishes.

Central to Confucian thought is the principle of *ren*, often translated as "humaneness" or "benevolence." *Ren* reflects an attitude of care and compassion toward others, rooted in the understanding that our lives are interconnected. "The man of *ren*," Confucius wrote, "wishing to establish himself, seeks also to establish others; wishing to enlarge himself, he seeks also to enlarge others." This teaching encourages us to recognize that our personal growth is inseparable from the well-being of those around us. By fostering connections built on empathy and mutual care, we create a ripple effect that strengthens families, communities, and societies.

While Aristotle and Confucius laid the philosophical groundwork for understanding human connection, modern psychology has provided scientific validation for its importance. Research consistently shows that belonging—a deep sense of being seen, valued, and connected— is one of the most fundamental human needs.

Psychologist Abraham Maslow, in his hierarchy of needs, positioned belonging just above basic physiological and safety needs. Without meaningful connection, individuals struggle to achieve higher states of growth, fulfillment, and self-actualization.

The consequences of disconnection are significant. Loneliness, described by former U.S. Surgeon General Dr. Vivek Murthy as an "epidemic," is linked to a range of negative health outcomes, including increased stress, depression, and even physical illness. Murthy's work highlights that loneliness is not simply an emotional state but a public health crisis—one that underscores the essential role of connection in human well-being. Studies show that people who have strong social relationships live longer, recover from illness more quickly, and report higher levels of happiness. Connection, it turns out, is as vital to our survival as food and water.

A powerful example of this truth comes from the longest-running study on human happiness, conducted by Harvard University over the course of 85 years. The study's findings are striking in their simplicity: the single most important factor in determining a person's happiness and health is the quality of their relationships. Wealth, status, and achievements matter far less than having people in our lives with whom we share love, trust, and connection. As one of the study's directors, Dr. Robert Waldinger, concluded, "Good relationships keep us happier and healthier. Period."

This wisdom, echoed across centuries and disciplines, invites us to reflect on our own lives: Are we prioritizing connection, or have we allowed busyness, distraction, or fear to create distance? In a world where technology offers constant communication but often little genuine connection, the challenge is to cultivate relationships that are real, meaningful, and nourishing. This begins with simple but intentional acts: reaching out to a friend, being fully present in conversations, or expressing gratitude to those who matter most. Connection thrives not in grand gestures but in small, consistent efforts to show up for one another.

The importance of human connection extends beyond personal relationships to the broader sense of community and belonging. Aristotle understood this, recognizing that individuals achieve their highest potential within a shared social structure. Modern communities—whether rooted in neighborhoods, workplaces, or shared interests—offer a sense of identity and support that strengthens both individuals and groups. When people feel connected to something larger than themselves, they experience greater purpose and resilience.

Consider the resilience of communities in times of hardship. After natural disasters or tragedies, it is often the bonds between individuals that provide the strength to rebuild. People come together to support one another, demonstrating the power of connection to transform suffering into hope. This phenomenon highlights a profound truth: when we face challenges together, we discover a shared strength that transcends individual limitations.

At its heart, the importance of human connection lies in its ability to remind us that we are not alone. It anchors us in a shared humanity, offering both comfort and inspiration. Aristotle, Confucius, and modern psychologists all converge on this point: connection is the thread that weaves meaning into our lives. It allows us to flourish, to heal, and to grow.

As we move forward, the invitation is clear: prioritize connection. Invest in relationships that uplift and nourish you. Seek out communities where you can both give and receive support. Embrace the truth that, as Confucius taught, our individual well-being is inseparable from the well-being of others. In doing so, we honor the power of connection—a power that enables us to thrive as individuals and as a collective whole.

Building Meaningful Relationships

Meaningful relationships lie at the heart of a fulfilling life, providing us with companionship, emotional support, and a sense of belonging. Yet cultivating such relationships requires intentionality, effort, and wisdom—qualities emphasized by thinkers throughout history. From Cicero's reflections on friendship to Montaigne's musings on connection and contemporary insights into the nature of bonds, building strong relationships is an art that transcends time.

Cicero, the Roman statesman and philosopher, offered one of the most enduring examinations of friendship in his work *De Amicitia* ("On Friendship"). For Cicero, true friendship was not built on utility or fleeting pleasure but on shared values, trust, and mutual respect. "Friendship," he wrote, "is nothing else than an accord in all things, human and divine, conjoined with mutual goodwill and affection." He viewed friendship as an essential part of a virtuous and happy life—one that nurtures the soul as much as it supports the individual.

Cicero identified honesty as the cornerstone of meaningful relationships. He argued that true friends must challenge one another, offering counsel even when it is difficult or uncomfortable. "The man who is afraid to tell his friend what is wrong does not deserve to call himself a friend," he wrote. To Cicero, friendship is not about blind agreement but about helping one another grow into the best versions of ourselves. This idea remains relevant today, particularly in an age where superficial interactions often replace genuine connection. A true friend is not someone who simply validates us but someone who is willing to tell us the truth with compas-

sion, pushing us toward growth and self-awareness.

The French philosopher Michel de Montaigne
expanded on this idea in his essays, particularly
in his reflections on his profound friendship with
Étienne de La Boétie. For Montaigne, the bond
between true friends was sacred—so rare and
extraordinary that it transcended the ordinary
connections of daily life. "In true friendship,"
he wrote, "souls mix and blend with each other
so completely that they efface the seam that
joined them." Montaigne's description speaks
to the depth of intimacy and trust that charac-
terizes the most meaningful relationships. True
friendship, he believed, creates a space where
individuals can reveal their innermost selves
without fear of judgment or rejection.

Montaigne's reflections also highlight the importance of reciprocity in building strong relationships. Friendship, like all meaningful bonds,
thrives on mutual giving and receiving. It is
not a transaction but an exchange of trust, care,
and understanding. This principle extends beyond friendships to familial and professional
connections, where reciprocity fosters trust and

strengthens bonds. Montaigne challenges us to reflect on our relationships: *Am I showing up fully for those I care about? Am I offering the same level of honesty, trust, and support that I seek in return?*

In today's world, where connection often feels fleeting and surface-level, these insights offer a timeless reminder: meaningful relationships require depth, vulnerability, and effort. Modern thinkers like psychologist Esther Perel have explored this truth, particularly in the context of romantic and familial relationships. Perel emphasizes the importance of "showing up" for those we love—not just physically but emotionally. In her view, relationships are strengthened through presence, curiosity, and intentional connection. She encourages individuals to ask deeper questions, to listen actively, and to express appreciation regularly. "Love rests on two pillars," Perel explains, "surrender and autonomy. Our need for togetherness exists alongside our need for separateness." This balance—of supporting others while honoring our individuality—allows relationships to thrive.

Similarly, building professional relationships

requires trust, integrity, and shared purpose. In his book *Leaders Eat Last,* author and leadership expert Simon Sinek explores how meaningful connections within organizations foster collaboration, loyalty, and success. Drawing on examples from the military and corporate world, Sinek argues that strong relationships are built on a foundation of trust and empathy. Leaders who prioritize relationships—who listen, support, and value their team members—create environments where individuals feel seen, respected, and inspired.

The workplace offers a unique opportunity to build connections that go beyond the transactional. Colleagues who invest in understanding one another's strengths, challenges, and aspirations create teams that are not only effective but deeply connected. Sinek's work invites us to ask: *Am I building relationships at work that are grounded in trust and mutual respect? Am I contributing to a culture of connection and support?*

The art of building meaningful relationships is also evident in the quiet, everyday moments of life. Consider the family gathering where generations share stories and laughter. The friend who shows up with a listening ear during a difficult time. The colleague who offers encouragement when we doubt ourselves. These moments, while small, are the building blocks of relationships that sustain us. They remind us that connection is not about grand gestures but about consistent, intentional acts of care and presence.

Practical wisdom for nurturing meaningful relationships begins with attention and effort. In a world of distractions, being fully present with others—putting aside phones, agendas, and anxieties—is one of the most powerful gifts we can offer. It also requires listening deeply, not merely to respond but to understand. Cicero's emphasis on honesty challenges us to engage in difficult conversations with kindness, recognizing that relationships grow stronger when built on trust and truth.

Vulnerability, as explored in the previous section, also plays a key role. Relationships deepen when we are willing to share our imperfections, fears, and dreams, creating space for others to do the same. In professional settings, this might mean admitting a mistake or asking for help. In personal relationships, it might mean expressing gratitude, apologizing sincerely, or sharing our innermost thoughts.

Finally, reciprocity ensures that relationships remain balanced and nourishing. Building meaningful connections requires mutual investment—showing up for others as we hope they will show up for us. Whether through a thoughtful message, an offer of help, or a moment of shared laughter, these small acts reinforce the bonds that sustain us.

In the end, building meaningful relationships is one of the most rewarding pursuits of a fulfilling life. Cicero, Montaigne, and contemporary thinkers remind us that such relationships do not happen by chance—they are cultivated through honesty, presence, and care. They challenge us to prioritize the connections that matter, to nurture friendships and bonds that enrich our lives and those of others.

When we invest in relationships, we honor a fundamental truth: that we are not meant to walk through life alone. It is through these connections—built on trust, reciprocity, and love—

that we find strength, meaning, and belonging. In building relationships that matter, we create not only a better life for ourselves but also a richer, more connected world for those around us.

Creating and Leading Communities

Communities are the bedrock of human civilization, bringing together individuals in pursuit of shared goals, mutual support, and a sense of belonging. Whether forged through neighborhoods, movements, workplaces, or global causes, strong communities unite people by creating a sense of purpose and collective identity. History's greatest leaders—visionaries like Mahatma Gandhi, alongside modern movements—demonstrate that communities do not emerge by accident. They are intentionally built, nurtured, and led with a focus on unity, shared values, and the belief that together we are far stronger than alone.

Mahatma Gandhi, often called the "father of the Indian independence movement," is one of the most powerful examples of someone who not only created but led a community that reshaped history. Gandhi understood that true leadership

lies not in commanding others but in serving
them and inspiring a shared vision. In the early
20th century, India faced the immense challenge
of colonial rule under the British Empire—a
system that divided and oppressed its people.
Gandhi recognized that India's freedom would
not come through violence or isolated resistance but through a united, peaceful movement
grounded in shared purpose.

Gandhi's leadership was defined by his ability
to foster unity across diverse communities. India,
a vast and multicultural country, was marked
by deep religious, cultural, and socioeconomic
divides. Yet Gandhi's vision transcended these
differences. He appealed to people's shared humanity, urging them to see themselves as part
of something larger—a collective force capable
of achieving independence through nonviolent
resistance. His philosophy of *ahimsa* (nonviolence) became the unifying principle of the
movement, teaching that strength is not found
in conflict but in steadfast, peaceful action. "You
may never know what results come of your
actions," Gandhi said, "but if you do nothing,
there will be no result."

Gandhi's Salt March of 1930 is a profound example of community-building in action. In protest of the British salt tax, which disproportionately harmed the poor, Gandhi led a 240-mile march to the Arabian Sea, where he and thousands of followers symbolically produced their own salt. What began as a seemingly simple act became a rallying cry for millions across India, uniting farmers, laborers, and intellectuals alike. The march demonstrated the power of a shared purpose to galvanize a community, inspiring people to stand together in pursuit of justice.

The lessons from Gandhi's leadership resonate far beyond his time. His approach teaches us that creating and leading communities begins with a clear, inclusive vision—one that inspires people to see themselves as part of a collective mission. Effective leaders create spaces where individuals feel seen, valued, and empowered to contribute to a shared goal. In today's world, this could mean uniting a team at work, organizing a grassroots movement, or fostering collaboration within a neighborhood. The principle remains the same: communities thrive when they are built on trust, shared purpose, and the belief that every voice matters.

Modern movements offer additional insights into the art of community-building. Consider the civil rights movement in the United States, led by figures like Martin Luther King Jr. Like Gandhi, King understood that a community united by shared values and peaceful action could overcome seemingly insurmountable challenges. His "I Have a Dream" speech, delivered in 1963, articulated a vision that transcended racial and socioeconomic boundaries, inviting people to join a movement that promised justice, equality, and dignity for all.

King's leadership was grounded in empathy, resilience, and the ability to inspire hope. He cultivated a community that was not defined by anger but by love and perseverance. "We must learn to live together as brothers," King said, "or perish together as fools." His words remind us that strong communities are built not through division but through connection—by recognizing the humanity we share and the common goals that unite us.

The rise of modern movements, such as climate activism and social justice initiatives, further highlights the role of community in addressing global challenges. Movements like Fridays for Future, led by young activists such as Greta Thunberg, demonstrate the power of collective action in a digital age. Through social media, people from diverse backgrounds have come together to advocate for environmental sustainability, proving that technology can amplify connection and purpose. These movements underscore a key principle: communities today are no longer bound by geography. Shared purpose, fueled by communication and collaboration, allows people to unite across borders to effect change.

Yet building and leading communities also requires vulnerability, humility, and adaptability. Leaders must recognize that communities are dynamic, evolving entities shaped by the contributions of every member. Effective leadership is not about exerting control but about empowering others to lead alongside you. It means creating environments where individuals feel safe to express their ideas, challenge assumptions, and take ownership of their roles within the collective.

Practical strategies for fostering strong communities begin with active listening and empathy. Leaders who listen to the needs, hopes, and challenges of their communities build trust and cultivate a sense of belonging. Whether leading a team, a social group, or a movement, this means asking: *What matters most to the people here? How can I create a space where everyone feels valued and heard?*

Equally important is the practice of shared purpose. Gandhi and King inspired movements because they articulated visions that resonated deeply with people's values and aspirations. In building communities, it is essential to define a unifying goal—one that transcends individual differences and inspires collective action. This could be as simple as improving communication within a workplace team or as ambitious as addressing global issues like poverty or climate change.

Finally, leading a community requires resilience. Challenges are inevitable, whether in the form of disagreements, setbacks, or external resistance. Gandhi's Salt March and King's nonviolent protests were met with opposition, yet their movements persevered because they remained anchored in their purpose. Resilient leaders guide their communities through difficulty by modeling hope, patience, and unwavering commitment.

At its essence, creating and leading communities is about bringing people together in pursuit of something greater than themselves. It is about fostering connection, trust, and shared purpose while empowering individuals to contribute their unique strengths. Gandhi, King, and modern movements demonstrate that communities, when united by a common goal, possess extraordinary power to transform lives and societies.

For those seeking to build communities — whether in families, workplaces, or global movements — the invitation is clear: lead with vision, empathy, and resilience. Cultivate spaces where people feel connected, valued, and inspired to act. In doing so, we honor a fundamental truth: that together, we are capable of achieving far more than we ever could alone.

The Role of Empathy and Compassion

At the heart of human connection lies a transformative power—empathy and compassion. These qualities allow us to bridge divides, foster understanding, and create a more harmonious world. While often viewed as virtues, empathy and compassion are far more than lofty ideals; they are practical tools that enhance personal and collective well-being. Rooted in ancient Buddhist philosophy and supported by modern psychology, they remind us that authentic connection flourishes not in judgment or self-interest but in the willingness to see, understand, and care for others.

Buddhism, a spiritual tradition that has shaped cultures for over 2,500 years, places empathy and compassion at the core of its teachings. The concept of *karuna*, which translates to "compassion," is seen as an essential practice for achieving both inner peace and communal harmony. The Buddha taught that suffering is a universal experience, shared by all living beings. By recognizing this shared vulnerability, we can cultivate compassion—not as pity but as a deep, genuine desire to alleviate the suffering of others. In doing so, we not only relieve pain but also transform our own hearts. "If your compassion does not include yourself," the Buddha added, "it is incomplete." Compassion, therefore, begins with empathy for ourselves and extends outward, connecting us to the broader human experience.

The Dalai Lama, one of the most prominent modern voices for compassion, expands on this teaching by framing compassion as an antidote to division. In his writings and speeches, he reminds us that empathy allows us to see others not as strangers or adversaries but as fellow human beings, each carrying joys, sorrows, and struggles. "Love and compassion are necessities, not luxuries," he says. "Without them, humanity cannot survive." The Dalai Lama's philosophy challenges us to move beyond judgment and cultivate a mindset of understanding—particularly toward those who are different from us. When we see others through the lens of compassion, barriers dissolve, and connection becomes possible.

Scientific research has provided further evidence of the profound impact empathy and compassion have on individual and collective well-being. Psychologists define empathy as the ability to understand and share the feelings of another, while compassion involves the active desire to alleviate their pain. Neuroscientific studies have revealed that acts of compassion activate reward centers in the brain, creating feelings of joy and satisfaction. In other words, helping others does not deplete us; it energizes and uplifts us.

Dr. Daniel Goleman, author of *Emotional Intelligence*, identifies empathy as a key component of strong relationships, effective leadership, and societal progress. Goleman describes three types of empathy: cognitive empathy, or understanding another's perspective; emotional empathy, or sharing their feelings; and compassionate empathy, which combines understanding and action. He argues that compassionate empathy is the most powerful form because it inspires us to respond to the needs of others rather than merely observing them. This insight highlights an important truth: empathy is not passive. It is an active force that invites us to care, to connect, and to act in ways that make a difference.

Empathy and compassion are also central to healing relationships and strengthening communities. In conflicts, whether personal or societal, it is often a lack of understanding that fuels division. When we fail to see the humanity in others, we create distance, misunderstanding, and resentment. Yet empathy allows us to step into another's experience, to see the world as they see it, and to recognize the emotions that drive their actions. This shift—simple yet profound—can dissolve anger, foster forgiveness, and create the foundation for reconciliation.

Consider the work of Nelson Mandela, who demonstrated the transformative power of empathy during South Africa's struggle to overcome apartheid. After spending 27 years imprisoned for resisting an oppressive system, Mandela emerged not with vengeance but with compassion and a vision for unity. He chose to see the humanity even in his oppressors, recognizing that hatred and division would only perpetuate suffering. "No one is born hating another person," Mandela said. "People must learn to hate, and if they can learn to hate, they can be taught to love." By leading with empathy and compassion, Mandela united a fractured nation, proving that understanding and connection are more powerful than conflict.

In our daily lives, empathy and compassion play equally vital roles. Relationships deepen when we truly listen to others—not merely hearing their words but seeking to understand their experiences and emotions. This requires presence, patience, and a willingness to let go of assumptions. When a friend shares their struggles, for example, our instinct may be to offer solutions or shift the conversation to our own experiences. Yet empathy asks us to pause, to listen, and to say, *"I see you. I hear you. I'm here with you."* In moments of hardship, this simple act of presence can be profoundly healing.

Compassion extends this practice further, inspiring us to take action in ways that alleviate suffering. This might mean offering help to a neighbor in need, supporting a coworker through a difficult time, or advocating for justice on behalf of those who are marginalized. Acts of compassion—no matter how small—create ripples that strengthen the fabric of our communities.

At the same time, cultivating compassion requires that we extend it inward. The Buddha's teaching on *metta*, or loving-kindness, emphasizes that compassion for others must begin with self-compassion. In a world that often equates vulnerability with weakness, many of us hold ourselves to impossibly high standards, judging our imperfections harshly. Yet self-compassion, as explored by psychologist Dr. Kristin Neff, is the foundation of resilience and well-being. By treating ourselves with the same kindness and understanding we offer others, we create space for growth, healing, and connection.

Practical strategies for cultivating empathy and compassion in daily life include active listening, perspective-taking, and mindfulness. Mindfulness practices, such as meditation, help us develop greater awareness of our emotions and the emotions of those around us. In Buddhist traditions, loving-kindness meditation involves silently repeating phrases of goodwill—first toward ourselves, then toward others, and finally toward all living beings. These practices train the mind to respond to the world with empathy and care, strengthening our capacity for connection.

In the end, the role of empathy and compassion in human connection cannot be overstated. They are the keys to understanding one another, healing divides, and building communities where everyone feels seen and valued. Buddhist philosophies and modern psychology converge on this truth: when we lead with empathy, we honor the shared humanity that unites us all.

The invitation, then, is to practice empathy and compassion as daily habits. Listen deeply. Seek to understand. Act with care and kindness, both toward yourself and others. As the Dalai Lama reminds us, "Be kind whenever possible. It is always possible." Through these simple yet profound practices, we transform not only our relationships but also the world around us—one connection at a time.

CHAPTER 7: REFLECTIONS ON MORTALITY – EMBRACING LIFE BY ACCEPTING DEATH

Philosophers on the Nature of Death

To accept death is to embrace life fully. The nature of mortality has preoccupied humanity since time immemorial, inspiring philosophers, poets, and spiritual leaders to explore its significance and to guide us toward peace in its inevitability. Figures like Socrates, Seneca, and the Buddha offer profound wisdom on how accepting death as a natural and essential part of existence allows us to overcome fear and live with deeper purpose. Their teachings remind us that death is not an enemy to be defeated but a truth to be understood—one that, far from diminishing life, enhances its beauty.

Socrates, often considered the father of Western philosophy, faced death with a calmness that has inspired countless generations. In *The Apology*, Plato recounts Socrates' trial and subsequent death sentence for "corrupting the youth" of Athens and challenging traditional beliefs. Despite being given the chance to save himself by abandoning his principles, Socrates chose to accept death rather than betray his pursuit of truth. His approach to mortality was rooted in a belief that death is not something to fear, for it is either a peaceful nothingness — "like a dreamless sleep" — or a transition to another existence where the soul continues its journey.

To Socrates, fearing death was irrational because it reflected an assumption of knowledge we do not possess. "To fear death, gentlemen, is no other than to think oneself wise when one is not," he declared to the Athenian court. His words challenge us to reflect on the nature of our fear: do we fear death because of its mystery, or because we cling to life without appreciating its impermanence? Socrates teaches us that death is simply part of the order of existence, no more unnatural than birth or aging. By accepting it, we free ourselves to live with courage, integrity, and authenticity, unburdened by the dread of what lies beyond.

Seneca, the Roman Stoic philosopher, expanded on Socratic ideas, offering a practical framework for confronting mortality. In his *Letters to Lucilius*, Seneca repeatedly emphasized that to fear death is to misunderstand life itself. For the Stoics, death is not an event to be postponed or resisted; it is part of the natural flow of existence, governed by forces beyond our control. Seneca argued that our time on earth is finite, and the key to living well lies in recognizing the value of every moment. "It is not that we have a short time to live," he wrote, "but that we waste a lot of it."

Seneca's philosophy encourages us to reframe our relationship with time. When we accept that death is inevitable, we begin to appreciate the gift of life more fully. Each day becomes an opportunity to align our actions with our values, to pursue what matters most, and to let go of trivial distractions. For Seneca, the wise individual is one who lives as though each day were their last—not with fear but with intentionality. "Let us prepare our minds as if we'd come to the very end of life," he advises. "Let us postpone nothing. Let us balance life's books each day." This practice of "memento mori," or remembering death, allows us to live with clarity and purpose, knowing that our time is precious.

Buddhist philosophy offers a similarly profound perspective on mortality, rooted in the teachings of the Buddha. Central to Buddhism is the understanding that impermanence (*anicca*) is a fundamental truth of existence. Everything in life—our bodies, relationships, possessions, and experiences—is transient, constantly arising and passing away. Clinging to the illusion of permanence leads to suffering, while accepting impermanence liberates us to live with mindfulness and equanimity.

The Buddha taught that by meditating on death, we free ourselves from attachment and cultivate gratitude for the present moment. This is not a morbid exercise but a path to enlightenment, one that allows us to see life with greater clarity. In the *Dhammapada*, the Buddha offers this reflection: "All conditioned things are impermanent—when one sees this with wisdom, one turns away from suffering." By accepting death as natural and inevitable, we can approach life without grasping, resentment, or denial. We learn to appreciate each breath, each connection, and each opportunity to live meaningfully.

One of the most powerful practices in Buddhism is the contemplation of one's mortality through mindfulness. In Tibetan traditions, practitioners reflect on death not as a distant abstraction but as a present reality. This practice, known as *Maranasati*, or mindfulness of death, encourages

individuals to face their mortality with acceptance and to use it as a source of motivation for
living authentically. It invites us to ask: *If this
were my last day, would I live it any differently?* By
embracing impermanence, we discover a deeper
sense of freedom and joy in the life we have.

These philosophical teachings converge on a
shared truth: death is not to be feared or denied
but accepted as an integral part of existence. Socrates teaches us to approach it with reason and
courage, Seneca urges us to live each day fully,
and the Buddha shows us how impermanence
can become a source of wisdom and liberation.
Together, they offer a powerful antidote to the
fear of mortality—an invitation to embrace life
with greater intention, clarity, and peace.

In practical terms, reflecting on death does not
diminish life but enriches it. It reminds us to
prioritize what truly matters: meaningful relationships, purposeful work, and the simple joys
that make life beautiful. When we accept that
our time is limited, we become more present,
more compassionate, and more courageous. We
let go of petty grievances and trivial distractions,
recognizing that every moment is a gift.

Consider the story of Japanese *sakura*, or cherry blossoms, which bloom briefly each spring before falling to the ground. In Japanese culture, the fleeting beauty of the blossoms symbolizes the transience of life—an elegant reminder of impermanence. By appreciating their brief existence, we come to understand the value of our own. The cherry blossom teaches us that life's beauty lies not in its duration but in its intensity and authenticity.

The wisdom of Socrates, Seneca, and the Buddha invites us to live in harmony with the truth of mortality. To accept death is not to surrender to despair but to awaken to life's fullness. It is a call to live boldly, to love deeply, and to approach each day with gratitude. As Seneca so eloquently reminds us, "He who has learned how to die has unlearned how to be a slave." In accepting death, we free ourselves to live—not in fear but in the radiant clarity of the present moment.

Living Fully Through Awareness of Mortality

When we embrace the reality of impermanence—our mortality and the fleeting nature of all things—we begin to live more intentionally, fully, and deeply. Awareness of death, far from casting a shadow over life, sharpens its beauty, inspiring us to savor each moment and prioritize what truly matters. The wisdom of Stoicism and Japanese Zen both emphasize that life's impermanence is not something to lament but a profound reminder to live deliberately, with presence and purpose.

The Stoics, ancient philosophers who embraced life's harsh realities with clarity and resolve, understood that the inevitability of death is a transformative teacher. Central to their philosophy is the practice of *memento mori*, a Latin phrase meaning "remember that you must die." For the Stoics, reflecting on mortality was not a morbid exercise but a way to cultivate gratitude, discipline, and perspective. Marcus Aurelius, Roman emperor and Stoic philosopher, often reflected on the fleeting nature of life in his *Meditations*, reminding himself: "You could leave life right now. Let that determine what you do and say and think."

This reminder—that death can come at any moment—does not lead to despair but to urgency. For Marcus Aurelius, awareness of mortality was a call to action. If time is short, then every moment matters. If life is uncertain, then we must not delay our efforts to live with integrity, purpose, and kindness. This perspective invites us to ask ourselves: *How am I spending the finite time I have? Am I living in alignment with my values, or am I squandering time on distractions and regrets?* In contemplating these questions, we reclaim our agency and infuse our days with intention.

Seneca, another prominent Stoic, described time as our most precious resource—a resource that cannot be replenished once spent. In *On the Shortness of Life*, he wrote, "It is not that we have a short time to live, but that we waste a lot of it." Seneca challenged his readers to recognize that life feels short only when we fail to use it well. His teachings encourage us to avoid trivial pursuits and to focus instead on meaningful activities: fostering relationships, contributing to society, and pursuing personal growth. By embracing the truth of impermanence, we become less tolerant of procrastination and more attuned to the richness of the present moment.

The Stoic practice of embracing mortality finds a powerful counterpart in Japanese Zen Buddhism, where the concept of impermanence (*anicca*) is a central tenet. Zen teaches that everything in life—our thoughts, emotions, relationships, and experiences—is transient, constantly arising and fading away. Like a river flowing continuously, nothing in the world is fixed or permanent. While this truth can initially provoke discomfort, it ultimately liberates us from attachment and allows us to appreciate life as it is.

A beautiful example of this philosophy is found in the Japanese tradition of *wabi-sabi*, which celebrates the beauty of imperfection, impermanence, and incompleteness. In the context of Zen, awareness of mortality is not about fixating on the end but about finding beauty in the fleeting nature of all things. A cherry blossom, or *sakura*, serves as a perfect metaphor for this wisdom. The delicate blossoms bloom for only a short time each spring before falling to the earth, their brief existence a poignant reminder of life's transience. Rather than mourning their impermanence, the Japanese culture reveres their fleeting beauty, seeing it as a reflection of life's fragile and precious nature.

Zen master Shunryu Suzuki echoes this sentiment in his teachings, reminding us to embrace the impermanence of life with mindfulness and presence. "Nothing exists except this present moment," he writes in *Zen Mind, Beginner's Mind*. "We cannot escape from this moment." Suzuki's words invite us to let go of regrets about the past and worries about the future, recognizing that life is lived only in the present. When we confront impermanence, we become more attuned to the beauty of everyday moments—a shared meal with loved ones, the warmth of sunlight on our skin, the simple joy of being alive.

One practical way to cultivate this awareness is through mindfulness—a practice deeply rooted in both Zen and modern psychology. Mindfulness encourages us to pay full attention to the present moment, to observe our thoughts and emotions without judgment, and to engage fully in whatever we are doing. Whether we are drinking tea, walking in nature, or speaking with a friend, mindfulness allows us to experience life with greater depth and clarity. By anchoring ourselves in the present, we become more aware of life's impermanence and more appreciative of its beauty.

The teachings of Stoicism and Zen converge on an essential truth: when we embrace the fleeting nature of life, we stop taking it for granted. We begin to see the ordinary as extraordinary, recognizing that even the simplest experiences are gifts to be cherished. A sunset becomes more vibrant when we remember that no two are ever the same. A conversation with a loved one carries more weight when we understand that life offers no guarantees of another. Impermanence, rather than diminishing life, magnifies its value.

The philosopher Alan Watts, whose work bridges Eastern and Western thought, described life's impermanence as a dance—one that is meaningful precisely because it does not last forever. "The more a thing tends to be permanent, the more it tends to be lifeless," Watts observed. He encouraged his readers to embrace life's flow, to stop clinging to what is already passing, and to participate fully in the unfolding present. By doing so, we move beyond fear and find joy in the impermanent beauty of existence.

Practical wisdom for living fully through awareness of mortality begins with simple but intentional acts. Reflecting on our impermanence reminds us to prioritize what brings us meaning: nurturing relationships, pursuing passions, and contributing to something larger than ourselves. It invites us to say what needs to be said, to forgive what needs to be forgiven, and to let go of trivial concerns that drain our time and energy. Each day becomes an opportunity to live with greater purpose, gratitude, and authenticity.

In the end, both the Stoics and Zen masters offer us a profound gift: the ability to live fully by accepting life's impermanence. Marcus Aurelius teaches us to let the knowledge of death inspire intentionality, while Zen reminds us to find beauty in the fleeting present. Together, they challenge us to ask: *If life is impermanent, how will I choose to live today?*

The answer lies in the awareness that life, though brief, is infinitely precious. When we embrace mortality, we reclaim the power to shape our days, to love without reservation, and to experience the richness of life in all its imperfection. By accepting that nothing lasts forever, we learn to cherish what we have—here, now, in this moment.

Overcoming the Fear of Death

To confront the fear of death is to confront the nature of existence itself. For many, the thought of death—of ceasing to be, of the unknown—can evoke deep anxiety and dread. Yet the greatest thinkers, from existential philosophers to Stoic sages, have offered powerful perspectives on reframing our fears. Figures like Martin Heidegger and Epictetus teach us that while the inevitability of death is unchangeable, our relationship with it is not. By confronting mortality with courage, clarity, and acceptance, we free ourselves from its shadow, reclaiming the ability to live more fully and authentically.

The German existentialist philosopher Martin Heidegger placed mortality at the very center of his philosophy, arguing that an awareness of death is what makes life meaningful. In his seminal work, *Being and Time*, Heidegger introduced the concept of *Being-toward-death*—a state of existence in which we fully recognize the reality of our mortality and allow it to shape how we live. To Heidegger, the avoidance of death leads to an inauthentic life, one in which we drift through existence passively, distracted by the mundane and the superficial. In contrast, confronting death awakens us to our freedom: the ability to choose how we live and to imbue our lives with purpose.

For Heidegger, the fear of death arises not from death itself but from our reluctance to accept its inevitability. He argued that society's tendency to hide death—by avoiding conversations about it or sanitizing its reality—only deepens our fear. "Death is not some distant event," Heidegger writes. "It is a constant possibility." Rather than running from this truth, he invites us to embrace it, for in doing so, we are freed to live authentically. Death becomes a reminder not of life's futility but of its urgency. It compels us to make deliberate choices, to live in alignment with what we value most, and to take responsibility for our existence.

The Stoic philosopher Epictetus offered a similar perspective, though with a practical and accessible approach. For Epictetus, death was not a source of fear because it lies outside our control. Central to Stoic philosophy is the dichotomy of control: there are things we can change and things we cannot. Death falls into the latter category. To waste time fearing what is inevitable, Epictetus argued, is to squander the precious time we do have. "I cannot escape death," he said, "but at least I can escape the fear of it."

Epictetus taught that the key to overcoming the fear of death lies in shifting our mindset. If we see death as unnatural or unjust, we will resist it, clinging to life with anxiety and desperation. But if we accept death as part of the natural order—no different than birth, growth, or aging—we can approach it with peace. "Why, then, do you fear death?" he asked. "It is no evil, for it is natural." Epictetus' wisdom reminds us that fear often stems from our perception of events rather than the events themselves. Death, when viewed through the lens of nature, loses its power to terrify.

The existential and Stoic approaches converge on a profound truth: the fear of death arises from an unwillingness to confront life's impermanence. By facing mortality directly, we strip it of its hold on us. This is not to say that the fear of death disappears entirely—Heidegger and Epictetus both recognized the natural human instinct to resist the unknown. But through reflection and acceptance, fear is replaced by clarity, and clarity allows us to live with greater intention.

A practical way to overcome the fear of death is to reframe it as a teacher rather than an adversary. Death's inevitability reminds us that our time is finite, and this knowledge can act as a powerful motivator. How often do we postpone our dreams, avoid difficult conversations, or delay meaningful action because we assume there will always be time? Reflecting on mortality forces us to ask: *What if time runs out? What would I regret not doing, not saying, or not becoming?* These questions, uncomfortable as they may be, illuminate what truly matters. They compel us to live with urgency and presence, treating each day as a gift.

The Roman emperor Marcus Aurelius, a devoted Stoic, practiced this philosophy daily. In his *Meditations*, he often reflected on the impermanence of life as a way of grounding himself in what was real and important. "You could leave life right now," he wrote. "Let that determine what you do and say and think." For Marcus, contemplating death was not a source of despair but of liberation. It freed him from trivial concerns and anchored him in the present moment. By accepting death, he discovered how to live more fully.

Modern psychology echoes these ancient insights, offering practical tools for reframing fears of mortality. Research into "terror management theory" suggests that much of human behavior—our pursuit of success, our desire for legacy, our avoidance of certain topics—is driven by an unconscious fear of death. Yet studies show that confronting mortality directly can reduce this fear. Practices like mindfulness, gratitude, and reflection help us accept life's impermanence and focus on what we can control: how we live, how we love, and how we contribute.

Mindfulness, in particular, offers a powerful antidote to the fear of death. By training our attention on the present moment, we learn to let go of anxieties about the future and regrets about the past. Death no longer looms as an abstract terror but becomes a natural part of the flow of life. As the Buddhist teacher Thich Nhat Hanh writes, "Our greatest fear is that when we die, we will become nothing. But if we look deeply, we will see that we continue in everything and everyone we touch." This perspective reminds us that death does not erase our existence but transforms it, connecting us to something larger than ourselves.

In confronting death, we discover that its greatest lesson is to live boldly and authentically. Heidegger teaches us to embrace the freedom that mortality affords, while Epictetus reminds us to let go of what we cannot control. Marcus Aurelius challenges us to make every moment count, and mindfulness grounds us in the beauty of the present. Together, these lessons offer a path not only to overcoming the fear of death but also to living with clarity, courage, and joy.

The invitation is clear: face death not with dread but with curiosity and acceptance. Let it be a guide, a motivator, and a teacher. In doing so, we reclaim the power to live—not in denial or avoidance but in the full, radiant light of our impermanence.

Leaving Nothing Unsaid

To live a life without regret is one of humanity's deepest aspirations, yet it remains elusive for many. Regret often stems not from the actions we take but from the words left unspoken and the opportunities allowed to slip away. Philosophers and thinkers across time have offered profound insights into life's brevity and the importance of leaving nothing unsaid — of embracing honesty, gratitude, and authenticity while there is still time. Figures like Marcus Aurelius, coupled with modern reflections, remind us that to live fully means expressing what lies in our hearts before the curtain falls.

Marcus Aurelius, the Roman emperor and Stoic philosopher, was intimately familiar with life's impermanence and the need to act without delay. In his *Meditations*, written as personal reflections rather than for public consumption, Marcus often pondered the fleeting nature of time. "Do not act as if you had ten thousand years to throw away," he urged himself. "Death hangs over you. While you live, while it is in your power, be good." These words reflect a crucial Stoic principle: the present moment is all we truly possess, and we must use it wisely.

For Marcus, this wisdom extended to how we interact with others. He recognized that death, unpredictable and inevitable, could claim anyone at any time. In light of this, he believed it was essential to treat every encounter as potentially the last. "When you kiss your child good night," he wrote, "whisper to yourself: they may not wake up. When you leave a friend, say goodbye with warmth, for you may not meet again." While this perspective may feel sobering, its purpose is not to burden us but to elevate our relationships. It is a call to live with intention, to express love, forgiveness, and appreciation while we still can.

The concept of leaving nothing unsaid challenges us to confront one of life's most common regrets: the failure to speak truthfully and lovingly to those who matter most. How often do we assume that we will have more time? That an apology, an expression of gratitude, or a declaration of love can wait until tomorrow? Yet the reality of mortality reminds us that tomorrow is never guaranteed. Those unspoken words—left locked away in fear, pride, or neglect—become heavy burdens we carry when it is too late to share them.

Modern reflections on this theme are perhaps best captured in the work of palliative care nurse Bronnie Ware, who documented the most common regrets of the dying. Among the most frequent was the lament: "I wish I had stayed in touch with people I care about." Ware's work highlights how easily we lose sight of what matters most—connection, forgiveness, and authentic expression—amid the distractions of daily life. The dying teach us what the living often forget: that our relationships define the quality of our lives, and leaving nothing unsaid is one of the greatest acts of love we can offer.

To live without regret begins with courage—the courage to be vulnerable, honest, and present. It requires us to let go of the fear that often holds us back: the fear of rejection, judgment, or discomfort. Yet when we allow these fears to dictate our actions, we risk sacrificing the very connections that give life meaning. The philosopher Jean-Paul Sartre famously said, "Man is condemned to be free," meaning that we are responsible for the choices we make, including the choice to speak or remain silent. If we wish to leave nothing unsaid, we must choose to act—to express what needs to be expressed, even when it feels uncomfortable or uncertain.

Consider the simple but profound power of an apology. How many relationships have been fractured because words of remorse were left unspoken? How many opportunities for healing have been lost because pride stood in the way? To apologize requires humility and courage, yet it can dissolve resentment and rebuild trust in ways that are deeply transformative. Likewise, expressing gratitude—telling someone what they mean to us, how they have shaped our lives—can be an act of extraordinary significance. We may assume that those we love already know how we feel, but unspoken gratitude, like unspoken love, can leave a void that only words can fill.

Leaving nothing unsaid also means confronting the reality of our own mortality. Reflecting on death is not morbid; it is clarifying. It allows us to recognize what truly matters and to prioritize the relationships and conversations that bring meaning to our lives. The Japanese Zen practice of *ichigo ichie*, often translated as "one time, one meeting," embodies this wisdom. It teaches that every moment is unique, never to be repeated, and should be approached as though it were the last. When we embrace this mindset, we become fully present in our interactions, savoring each conversation and ensuring that nothing important is left unsaid.

Practical wisdom for living without regret begins with small, intentional acts. It means reaching out to the friend we have lost touch with, expressing gratitude to the mentor who shaped our path, or telling our family members how much we love them. It means choosing to forgive—not for the other person's sake but for our own peace of mind. Forgiveness, like love, is a gift we give both to others and to ourselves.

It also means recognizing that honesty and authenticity are not luxuries but necessities. Too often, we withhold our truth out of fear or a desire to please others. Yet living authentically— speaking our minds and sharing our hearts—

frees us from the burden of regret. As Marcus Aurelius reminds us, "The happiness of your life depends upon the quality of your thoughts." To speak truthfully and kindly is to honor both ourselves and those around us.

In the end, leaving nothing unsaid is a commitment to living with integrity and presence. It is a vow to express love, gratitude, and truth while we still can. Mortality, rather than casting a shadow over life, illuminates its beauty and fragility. It reminds us that the time to act is now—not tomorrow, not someday, but this moment.

Let us, then, live as though every encounter is our last. Let us say what needs to be said, mend what needs to be mended, and celebrate the people we cherish. In doing so, we ensure that when the final chapter comes, we can look back not with regret but with peace, knowing that we left nothing unsaid. For as the poet Mary Oliver so poignantly asked, "Tell me, what is it you plan to do with your one wild and precious life?" The answer, perhaps, begins with the courage to speak, to love, and to live fully—before it is too late.

CHAPTER 8: THE LEGACY WE LEAVE – LESSONS ON CONTRIBUTION AND IMPACT

Defining Legacy Through Timeless Teachings

Legacy is often misunderstood as the pursuit of fame, fortune, or recognition that endures beyond our lifetime. Yet for the wisest thinkers and leaders throughout history, legacy was not measured in applause or monuments but in the meaningful contributions we make to others. To live a life of impact is not to seek immortality in the memories of strangers but to leave the world a little better, kinder, or more just than we found it. Philosophers like Confucius and Marcus Aurelius remind us that a legacy is not what we take with us when we are gone but what we leave behind—through our actions, our values, and the lives we touch along the way.

Confucius, the revered Chinese philosopher, taught that the foundation of a lasting legacy lies in virtue and service to others. For Confucius, an honorable life was built upon the principles of *ren* (benevolence), *li* (proper conduct), and *xiao* (filial piety). These virtues, he believed, not only elevated the individual but also created harmony within families, communities, and societies. "To be able, under all circumstances,

to practice five things constitutes perfect virtue,"
he said. "These five are gravity, generosity of
soul, sincerity, earnestness, and kindness."

Confucius' vision of legacy was not grandi-
ose. It did not rest on achievements inscribed
in history books but on the small, cumulative
acts that ripple outward—how we treat others,
how we guide future generations, and how we
uphold values that outlive us. He emphasized
that character and virtue are contagious; when
we embody integrity, kindness, and humility,
we inspire others to do the same. In this way, a
legacy is built not through words but through
example. "The superior man," Confucius wrote,
"thinks of virtue; the small man thinks of comfort." To Confucius, the true measure of a life
well-lived was not how much one amassed but
how much one gave.

Marcus Aurelius, the Roman emperor and Stoic
philosopher, similarly viewed legacy through
the lens of meaningful action rather than glory.
As leader of one of the most powerful empires
in history, Marcus could have easily been consumed by the pursuit of personal fame. Yet in
his private writings, collected in *Meditations*, he

grappled with questions of mortality, purpose, and the nature of legacy. "Consider how quickly all things are dissolved and resolved," he wrote, reflecting on the impermanence of life. "Only what you do now, and what you do with virtue, will matter in the end."

Marcus Aurelius rejected the illusion of eternal remembrance. He observed that even the greatest emperors, warriors, and thinkers would eventually be forgotten, their names eroded by time. What mattered, he argued, was not how long one's deeds were remembered but how well one lived according to reason, virtue, and justice. "Waste no more time arguing what a good man should be," he implored himself. "Be one." These words capture a profound truth: legacy is not about how we are remembered but about who we choose to be in this moment, for the benefit of others.

For Marcus, leaving a legacy was an act of quiet, consistent service to humanity. His Stoic teachings remind us that we cannot control how we are remembered, but we can control how we live. The key lies in focusing on what is within our power: our actions, our choices, and our interactions. When we act with integrity, compassion, and resilience, we contribute to a better world—regardless of whether our names are ever celebrated. This perspective invites us to shift our focus from ambition to contribution, from self-centered pursuits to meaningful impact.

The lessons of Confucius and Marcus Aurelius converge on a timeless truth: our legacy is not a monument we build for ourselves but a reflection of how we shape the lives of others. It is found in the child we inspire, the friend we comfort, the stranger we help, and the values we pass on. This understanding liberates us from the fear of obscurity and the relentless chase for recognition. Instead, it grounds us in the present, reminding us that every day is an opportunity to create a legacy of kindness, wisdom, and service.

Modern reflections on legacy echo these ancient teachings. The writer and theologian Albert Schweitzer once observed, "The only ones among you who will be really happy are those who have sought and found how to serve." Schweitzer's words remind us that a meaningful legacy is built through service—not necessarily through grand gestures but through small, intentional acts that improve the lives of others. Whether it is through mentorship, acts of kindness, or contributions to our communities, our impact is measured not in scale but in sincerity.

Practical wisdom for defining legacy begins with reflection. What values do we hold most dear? What kind of person do we wish to be remembered as—not by the world, but by the people closest to us? These questions challenge us to clarify our priorities and align our actions with our ideals. Confucius and Marcus Aurelius would remind us that a life of virtue and service requires no recognition to be significant. It is the quiet legacy of a life lived well—of a heart that loves, a mind that learns, and hands that give.

Legacy is also an ongoing process, not a final outcome. It is not something we create at the end of our lives but something we build in the small, ordinary moments of every day. The way we treat those around us, the care we show to our families, the wisdom we share with our communities—all of these become threads in the tapestry of our legacy. As the poet Maya

Angelou beautifully wrote, "People will forget what you said, people will forget what you did, but people will never forget how you made them feel." In this sense, our legacy lives on in the hearts of others—in the love, kindness, and inspiration we leave behind.

Ultimately, defining legacy is about embracing our capacity to make a difference. It is not reserved for heroes, leaders, or saints; it is available to all of us. Whether through a kind word, a helping hand, or a commitment to living authentically, we leave our mark on the world in ways we may never fully see. Like ripples in a pond, our actions extend far beyond ourselves, touching lives in ways both profound and invisible.

Confucius, Marcus Aurelius, and modern thinkers remind us that legacy is not about seeking immortality but about leaving a lasting impact—an impact defined not by accolades but by the quiet contributions that enrich the lives of others. As we reflect on what we wish to leave behind, we are called to live with intention, integrity, and purpose. For in the end, the greatest legacy we can leave is a life lived fully, with love, courage, and the humble desire to make the world a little better than we found it.

Acts of Service and Kindness

The legacy of a life well-lived is often written not in grand achievements or public acclaim but in the quiet, compassionate acts of service that ripple outward, shaping the lives of others. Figures like Mother Teresa and Albert Schweitzer remind us that even the smallest acts of kindness can leave a profound and lasting impact. Through their lives and teachings, we are inspired to see service not as an obligation but as a calling—a way to connect with others and contribute to a world where compassion prevails over indifference.

Mother Teresa, now Saint Teresa of Calcutta, exemplified the power of selfless service. Born in 1910 in what is now North Macedonia, she dedicated her life to caring for the poorest and most marginalized individuals. Her work began with the Missionaries of Charity, a congregation she founded in 1950 to serve "the hungry, the naked, the homeless, the crippled, the blind, the lepers, all those people who feel unwanted, unloved, and uncared for." For decades, Mother Teresa worked tirelessly to provide food, shelter, and dignity to those in need, often at great personal sacrifice.

What made Mother Teresa's legacy extraordinary was not only the scale of her work but the philosophy that guided it. She believed that true service lay in recognizing the inherent dignity of every person, regardless of their circumstances. "Not all of us can do great things," she famously said, "but we can do small things with great love." This perspective reframes service as something accessible to everyone. One need not be a saint or a hero to make a difference; even the simplest acts of kindness—offering a smile, listening to someone's pain, or sharing what we have—carry immense value.

Albert Schweitzer, the theologian, physician, and Nobel Peace Prize laureate, echoed this belief in his own life and work. Born in 1875 in Germany, Schweitzer pursued careers in theology, music, and medicine before dedicating himself to humanitarian work. In 1913, he founded a hospital in Lambaréné, Gabon, where he spent much of his life providing medical care to underserved communities. Schweitzer's philosophy, rooted in the concept of "reverence for life," emphasized the interconnectedness of all living beings and the moral imperative to alleviate suffering wherever possible.

Schweitzer's legacy demonstrates that service is not confined to any one field or profession. Whether through medicine, teaching, advocacy, or simple acts of care, we all have the capacity to contribute meaningfully to the well-being of others. "The purpose of human life," he wrote, "is to serve, and to show compassion and the will to help others." Like Mother Teresa, Schweitzer understood that the impact of service lies not in its scale but in its sincerity. It is the intention behind our actions—the love, empathy, and humility we bring to them—that creates lasting change.

These examples invite us to reflect on what it means to serve and why acts of kindness matter so deeply. Service is not only about addressing material needs; it is also about fostering connection and reminding others of their worth. In a world that often feels fractured and isolating, even the smallest gestures can reaffirm our shared humanity. A kind word, a helping hand, or a moment of genuine attention can be transformative, not only for the recipient but also for the giver.

Modern research in psychology supports this idea, showing that acts of kindness benefit both the individual performing them and the wider community. Studies have found that helping others releases endorphins, often referred to as the "helper's high," which improves mood and reduces stress. Moreover, acts of service strengthen social bonds, fostering trust, cooperation, and resilience within communities. These findings reinforce what Mother Teresa and Schweitzer understood intuitively: that kindness is a gift that enriches both the giver and the receiver.

One of the most powerful aspects of service is its ripple effect. When we extend kindness to others, we inspire them to do the same, creating a chain of positive actions that extends far beyond our immediate reach. Consider the story of a young boy who, after receiving a scholarship funded by anonymous donors, went on to become a teacher and mentor. The initial act of generosity not only changed his life but also influenced countless others through his work. This is the essence of legacy: the ability to create lasting impact through acts that may seem small or unnoticed in the moment.

Yet the transformative power of kindness lies not only in grand narratives but also in the ordinary moments of everyday life. Holding the door for a stranger, offering a compliment, or checking in on a friend—these simple gestures remind us that service does not require extraordinary effort. It requires only a willingness to see others, to acknowledge their struggles, and to act with empathy. In this way, kindness becomes both a habit and a way of being, shaping the world one moment at a time.

Service also challenges us to step outside ourselves and confront the larger issues facing humanity. While individual acts of kindness are invaluable, they are often amplified when combined with collective action. From grassroots movements to community initiatives, history is filled with examples of people coming together to address inequality, injustice, and suffering. These efforts remind us that service is not only

about helping individuals but also about contributing to systems and structures that uplift
entire communities.

Ultimately, the legacies of Mother Teresa and
Albert Schweitzer teach us that acts of service
and kindness are not just about improving the
world for others; they are also about becoming
the best versions of ourselves. In serving others,
we cultivate qualities like humility, empathy,
and gratitude. We learn to see beyond our own
needs and to recognize the interconnectedness
of all life. This is the paradox of service: by giving of ourselves, we grow richer in spirit.

The invitation, then, is to begin where we are.
Service does not require wealth, power, or extraordinary talent. It requires only an open heart
and a willingness to act. Whether by volunteer-
ing in our communities, supporting a friend in
need, or simply showing kindness in our daily
interactions, we all have the ability to make a
difference. As Schweitzer reminds us, "Even if
it is a little thing, do something for those who
have need of help, something for which you get
no pay but the privilege of doing it."

In the end, acts of service and kindness are the threads that weave the fabric of our legacy. They remind us that our greatest impact is not measured in accolades but in the lives we touch. Like ripples in a pond, our actions extend outward, creating a world that is gentler, kinder, and more compassionate. This, perhaps, is the true measure of a life well-lived: not what we accomplish for ourselves, but what we give to others.

Creating Meaningful Work

Our work is one of the most visible ways we leave a mark on the world. Whether through art, invention, teaching, or caregiving, the work we choose to do—and the spirit with which we approach it—has the power to shape not only our legacy but also the lives of others. Throughout history, great minds like Leonardo da Vinci have demonstrated the profound impact of meaningful work, inspiring us to see our labor not merely as a means to an end but as a vessel for purpose, creativity, and contribution.

Leonardo da Vinci's life exemplifies the potential of meaningful work to transcend time and place. Born in 1452, da Vinci was not just an artist but also an inventor, engineer, and scientist—a true polymath whose curiosity knew no bounds. His work, from the enigmatic *Mona Lisa* to his visionary sketches of flying machines, reflected a deep engagement with the mysteries of the natural world and the human condition. For Leonardo, work was not a task to be endured but a pursuit of wonder and understanding. He saw art, science, and innovation as interconnected expressions of the same universal truths.

What made Leonardo's legacy so enduring was not merely his talent but his mindset. He approached every project with meticulous attention to detail and a relentless curiosity. In his notebooks, he filled pages with questions—about the flow of water, the anatomy of the human body, the motion of birds. This habit of inquiry was central to his work's impact, reminding us that meaningful work begins with a sense of purpose and a commitment to discovery. "Learning never exhausts the mind," Leonardo wrote, a testament to his belief that work is most fulfilling when it arises from genuine passion and curiosity.

The lessons of Leonardo da Vinci extend far beyond the Renaissance. His life invites us to reflect on what makes our own work meaningful. While few of us may paint masterpieces or design flying machines, we all have the capacity to bring purpose and creativity to our labor. Meaningful work is not defined by fame or complexity but by the value it adds—to ourselves, to others, and to the world. It is work that aligns with our values, challenges us to grow, and contributes to something greater than ourselves.

The philosopher Aristotle offered similar insights, emphasizing that meaningful work is rooted in the pursuit of excellence and the fulfillment of our potential. In his *Nicomachean Ethics*, Aristotle argued that the highest human good, or *eudaimonia*—often translated as "flourishing"—is achieved through the active expression of our virtues in work and life. To Aristotle, work was not merely a means of survival but a domain in which we could cultivate our character and contribute to the well-being of others.

Aristotle's philosophy challenges us to view work not as a burden but as an opportunity for self-expression and service. He reminds us that the true value of our labor lies not in its material rewards but in its ability to bring out the best in us and to enhance the lives of those around us. This perspective encourages us to seek work that resonates with our passions and principles, and to approach even the most mundane tasks with care and intention.

Meaningful work also requires resilience and adaptability—qualities exemplified by countless innovators and creators throughout history. The painter Vincent van Gogh, for instance, struggled with rejection and financial hardship throughout his life, yet he continued to create with passion and authenticity. Though unappreciated in his time, his work now stands as a testament to the transformative power of persistence and belief in one's vision. Van Gogh's story reminds us that the impact of our work is not always immediate or visible. Often, its true significance emerges over time, in ways we cannot foresee.

In the modern world, meaningful work is increasingly associated with purpose-driven careers—roles that address social, environmental, or humanitarian challenges. From educators shaping young minds to scientists developing sustainable technologies, purpose-driven work exemplifies the idea that our labor can be a force for good. Yet meaningful work need not be limited to specific fields or professions. A barista who greets customers with warmth and kindness, a carpenter who takes pride in their craftsmanship, or a caregiver who offers comfort and dignity to the elderly—all of these contribute to a legacy of service and excellence.

To create meaningful work, we must first ask ourselves: What drives us? What values do we wish to embody in our labor? And how can we use our skills and passions to make a positive impact? These questions help us align our efforts with our deeper purpose, ensuring that our work reflects not only our abilities but also our ideals.

At the same time, meaningful work requires a willingness to embrace imperfection and uncertainty. Leonardo da Vinci, for all his brilliance, left many projects unfinished—not out of failure but because his curiosity often led him in new directions. This aspect of his legacy reminds us that the process of creation is just as important as the outcome. Meaningful work is not about achieving perfection but about engaging wholeheartedly in the act of doing, learning, and growing.

In our own lives, the pursuit of meaningful work need not be grand or extraordinary. It can be as simple as finding joy in the tasks we perform, seeking opportunities to help others, and approaching our labor with integrity and care. When we bring intention to our work—no matter its nature—we transform it into a source of fulfillment and impact. As the poet Khalil Gibran wrote in *The Prophet*, "Work is love made visible." These words remind us that the essence of meaningful work lies not in its external recognition but in the love, passion, and purpose we pour into it.

Ultimately, creating meaningful work is about leaving a legacy that reflects who we are and what we stand for. It is about using our talents and energy to contribute to a world that is better, kinder, and more just. Whether through art, innovation, service, or simple acts of care, our work becomes a testament to our values and a gift to future generations.

Leonardo da Vinci's legacy teaches us to approach our work with curiosity, creativity, and a commitment to excellence. Aristotle reminds us that work is a pathway to flourishing, a means of expressing our virtues and enriching the lives of others. Together, they inspire us to view our labor not as a chore but as a calling—a way to create, connect, and contribute.

As we reflect on the role of work in our lives, let us remember that its true meaning lies not in what we achieve but in what we give. Through purposeful, meaningful work, we shape not only our own lives but also the world we leave behind. And in that, we find the essence of legacy: the quiet, enduring impact of a life lived with intention, passion, and purpose.

Your Legacy Begins Now

Legacy is often spoken of as something we leave behind, a summation of our life's work and impact that becomes evident only when we are gone. Yet this perspective overlooks a vital truth: our legacy is not built in some distant future but in the choices we make today. Each moment offers an opportunity to shape the world around us, to influence others, and to act in ways that reflect our deepest values. By approaching life with intention, cultivating meaningful relationships, and embracing a mindset of contribution, we can begin building a legacy now—one that reflects who we are and the difference we wish to make.

The first step in building a legacy is to clarify what matters most to us. This requires reflection on our values, priorities, and aspirations. As the philosopher Socrates famously said, "The unexamined life is not worth living." To examine our lives is to ask: What do I want to stand for? What principles guide my actions? What kind of impact do I wish to have on those around me? These questions invite us to align our daily choices with our larger vision, ensuring that our actions reflect the person we aspire to be.

Building a legacy also requires us to recognize the power of small, consistent actions. While grand achievements and transformative events may leave a mark, it is often the quiet, everyday moments that define our legacy. A kind word, a thoughtful gesture, or a willingness to listen can have a profound impact on others, even if we do not see it immediately. The novelist Maya Angelou captured this idea beautifully when she said, "People will forget what you said, people will forget what you did, but people will never forget how you made them feel." This sentiment reminds us that our legacy is not just about what we accomplish but about how we treat others and the memories we create with them.

One of the most powerful ways to begin building a legacy is through our relationships. The connections we form—with family, friends, colleagues, and even strangers—are often where our greatest impact lies. Marcus Aurelius, the Stoic philosopher and Roman emperor, understood this well. In his *Meditations*, he reflected on the importance of living in harmony with others, treating them with kindness and fairness, and contributing to the common good. "What we do now echoes in eternity," he wrote, underscoring the idea that our actions, particularly those that influence others, have a ripple effect far beyond what we can see.

Cultivating meaningful relationships requires effort and intention. It means prioritizing the people we care about, being present in our interactions, and showing empathy and support. It also means addressing conflicts with humility and seeking to repair broken connections where possible. By investing in our relationships, we not only enrich our own lives but also create a network of influence and support that extends our impact. The love, wisdom, and encouragement we offer to others become part of their journey, continuing to resonate long after we are gone.

In addition to relationships, our mindset plays a crucial role in shaping our legacy. A mindset of contribution—a focus on giving rather than taking—allows us to see opportunities to make a difference in every situation. This does not mean ignoring our own needs or sacrificing our well-being; rather, it means approaching life with a spirit of generosity and collaboration. When we adopt this perspective, our actions are guided by the question: How can I add value to the world around me?

Consider the example of Mahatma Gandhi, whose legacy of nonviolence and social change was rooted in his unwavering commitment to service. Gandhi's philosophy was simple yet profound: by dedicating ourselves to causes larger than ourselves, we find purpose and fulfillment. "The best way to find yourself," he said, "is to lose yourself in the service of others." Gandhi's life reminds us that legacy is not about accumulating wealth or power but about dedicating our talents and energy to creating a better world.

For many, the path to building a legacy begins with identifying ways to contribute through their work or passions. Whether through art, innovation, education, or community service, our work can be a powerful vehicle for impact. As discussed earlier, the polymath Leonardo da Vinci exemplified how curiosity and creativity can leave a lasting imprint. Yet even in the most routine or modest roles, we can find opportunities to make a difference. A teacher who inspires their students, a nurse who offers comfort to patients, or a writer who shares their truth—all of these acts, no matter how small, contribute to a legacy of meaning and purpose.

Ultimately, the key to building a legacy is to start where we are, with what we have. It is easy to become overwhelmed by the idea of legacy, to feel that we must achieve something extraordinary or leave a mark that will be re-membered for centuries. Yet history is filled with examples of people whose quiet, unassum-ing actions created ripples of change. The civil rights leader Rosa Parks, for instance, made her stand not through grand gestures but through a single, resolute decision—to remain seated on a bus. Her courage, rooted in her everyday life, sparked a movement that transformed the course of history.

This perspective liberates us from the pressure to achieve perfection or recognition. It reminds us that our legacy is not a destination but a journey—a series of choices, interactions, and moments that collectively define who we are. By focusing on the present and acting with in-tention, we can create a legacy that reflects our values and aspirations.

As we reflect on our legacy, let us remember that it is not something we leave behind only at the end of our lives. It is something we build each day, in the way we live, love, and contrib-ute. Our actions, no matter how small, have the power to create ripples that extend far beyond what we can imagine. By embracing this truth, we reclaim the ability to shape our own story and to leave the world a little better than we found it.

Today is the perfect time to begin. The conversations we have, the choices we make, and the kindness we offer are all opportunities to create a legacy of compassion, integrity, and purpose. For as the poet Rumi wrote, "Try not to resist the changes that come your way. Instead, let life live through you. And do not worry that your life is turning upside down. How do you know that the side you are used to is better than the one to come?" In embracing life fully, we embrace our power to shape the legacy we leave—a legacy that begins, always, in the here and now.

CONCLUSION: EMBRACING THE JOURNEY OF A MEANINGFUL LIFE

As this journey through the wisdom of great minds comes to a close, it is worth pausing to reflect on the threads that tie together the themes we have explored. From love and happiness to resilience, authenticity, connection, and legacy, this book has sought to illuminate the timeless principles that shape a meaningful life. These principles, distilled from the teachings of history's most profound thinkers and leaders, remind us that the path to fulfillment is not a distant ideal but a journey we can embark on every day.

At its core, the message of this book is simple yet profound: our lives are defined by the choices we make, the values we uphold, and the connections we nurture. While external circumstances may shape the contours of our experience, it is ultimately our mindset, actions, and relationships that determine the quality and purpose of our existence. The lessons we draw from philosophers, visionaries, and changemakers teach us not only how to navigate life's challenges but also how to live with intention, courage, and grace.

Revisiting the Wisdom of Love and Connection

We began this journey by exploring the pursuit of love and the power of connection. From Plato's reflections on the nature of love to the teachings of Marcus Aurelius on empathy and trust, the message is clear: love in its many forms—romantic, familial, and universal—is a unifying force that gives life meaning.

Love is not a passive experience; it is an active choice to cultivate compassion, understanding, and presence in our relationships. Whether through acts of self-love that strengthen our foundation or the bonds we build with others, love is the thread that weaves our lives together. In a world that often feels fragmented, the practice of love and connection is a radical act of courage—one that reaffirms our shared humanity and reminds us that we are never truly alone.

The Art of Happiness and the Resilience of the Human Spirit

Happiness, as we have seen, is not a fleeting emotion but a state of being that arises from living in alignment with our values and embracing life's impermanence. The wisdom of the Stoics, Zen practitioners, and modern thinkers teaches us that true contentment is found not in external achievements but in the cultivation of gratitude, mindfulness, and perspective.

Similarly, resilience is not the absence of struggle but the ability to rise in the face of adversity. The stories of historical figures like Nelson Mandela and Helen Keller remind us that suffering, while inevitable, can be a powerful teacher. It is through resilience that we discover our strength, grow in character, and find meaning in even the most difficult circumstances. By accepting life's challenges with grace, we transform obstacles into opportunities for growth, reaffirming our capacity to endure and thrive.

Living Authentically and Embracing Mortality

To live authentically is to have the courage to be ourselves in a world that often pressures us to conform. The teachings of Socrates, Nietzsche, and contemporary thinkers like Brené Brown remind us that authenticity is not about perfection but about vulnerability and self-awareness. It is about embracing our flaws, honoring our unique journey, and living in alignment with our truth.

Mortality, though often feared, offers profound wisdom for those willing to confront it. As Marcus Aurelius and the Buddha teach, the awareness of death is not a source of despair but a clarion call to live fully. By accepting the impermanence of life, we are freed to focus on what truly matters: love, connection, and contribution. Each moment becomes an opportunity to leave nothing unsaid, to act with intention, and to create a life that reflects our deepest values.

Building a Legacy of Impact and Contribution

Finally, we explored the concept of legacy—not as a pursuit of fame or recognition but as the lasting impact of our actions, relationships, and contributions. Figures like Mother Teresa, Albert Schweitzer, and Leonardo da Vinci demonstrate that legacy is not reserved for the extraordinary; it is accessible to all who approach life with purpose and care.

Legacy begins in the present, in the small acts of kindness and service that ripple outward, touching lives in ways we may never fully see. It is built through meaningful work, authentic relationships, and a commitment to leaving the world a little better than we found it. As we embrace the idea that our legacy is a reflection of how we live, we are inspired to act with greater intention and to cherish the opportunities we have to make a difference.

Carrying the Lessons Forward

As you turn the final page of this book, consider the insights that resonate most deeply with you. Perhaps it is the call to embrace love with open arms, to cultivate gratitude for life's simple joys, or to confront adversity with courage and resilience. Perhaps it is the reminder to live authentically, to honor the fleeting beauty of each moment, or to begin building your legacy today through acts of kindness and service.

Whatever lessons speak to your heart, know that they are not abstract ideals but practical tools for shaping your journey. You do not need to be perfect or extraordinary to apply these principles; you need only to be willing—to take the first step, to reflect on your values, and to act with intention.

In the words of the poet Mary Oliver, "Tell me, what is it you plan to do with your one wild and precious life?" This question is not a challenge to achieve greatness but an invitation to live with purpose. It is a reminder that the choices we make, no matter how small, have the power to shape our story and to create a ripple effect of impact and meaning.

An Invitation to Begin

As you close this chapter, remember that the journey does not end here. The wisdom of history's great minds is not a destination but a guide—a compass to help you navigate the complexities of life with clarity and courage. Each day is an opportunity to begin again, to align your actions with your values, and to contribute to the world in ways that matter to you.

Whether through love, resilience, authenticity, or service, the path to a meaningful life is one you create with every step you take. By embracing the lessons of this book, you have the power to shape not only your own story but also the lives of those around you.

So let this be your call to action: live with intention, love with courage, and leave a legacy that reflects the best of who you are. For in the end, it is not the years we count but the moments we cherish, the lives we touch, and the impact we leave behind.

Your journey begins now. The next chapter is yours to write.

ACKNOWLEDGEMENT

Creating this book has been a deeply meaningful journey, one that would not have been possible without the support, wisdom, and inspiration of so many.

To the timeless thinkers and visionaries whose ideas form the foundation of this work, thank you for leaving a legacy that continues to illuminate the path of those who follow. Your courage to question, to seek, and to teach has been a guiding light in shaping this book.

To my friends, family, and community, your encouragement and belief in this project have been a source of strength and motivation. I am especially grateful to those who shared their insights and feedback, helping me to refine and elevate this work.

Finally, to the readers, thank you for joining me on this exploration of life's deepest questions. Your willingness to engage with these ideas brings them to life, and it is my hope that this book serves as a companion and guide on your own journey.

With heartfelt gratitude,
Felix Grayson

ABOUT THE AUTHOR

Felix Grayson's journey into timeless wisdom began in childhood, captivated by the stories of philosophers, leaders, and visionaries who shaped the way we think and live. Growing up in a home filled with books, he spent countless hours exploring ideas that asked life's biggest questions—a curiosity that would later define his work.

After facing his own modern challenges—balancing ambition, uncertainty, and the search for meaning—Felix discovered that the wisdom of the past offers profound guidance for the present. This realization became the foundation for the *Stoned Philosopher* series: a collection dedicated to translating ancient insights into practical lessons for today's world.

Felix's writing is more than reflection—it's an invitation to dialogue with history's greatest minds. Through each book, he helps readers find clarity, resilience, and purpose in their own lives—one timeless idea at a time.

When not writing, Felix enjoys quiet contemplation, deep conversation, and exploring the endless pursuit of wisdom in everyday moments.